THE FUTURE OF FINANCE IS NOW

The Most Important Trends in Finance for the Coming Decade Have Already Started

JASON SCHENKER

THE FUTURE OF FINANCE IS NOW

The Most Important Trends in Finance for the Coming Decade Have Already Started

BY JASON SCHENKER

ISBN: 978-1-946197-34-4 *Paperback*
     978-1-946197-33-7 *Ebook*

For my loving wife, Ashley.

CONTENTS

CONTENTS

LOOKING AHEAD

There's an old joke about two economists sitting by a campfire. A bear hops out of the woods, and one economist takes off running while the other puts on his running shoes.

The economist who started running away without shoes on says, "You'll never be able to outrun the bear with those on." To which the economist lacing up says, "I don't have to outrun the bear. I just have to outrun you."

And so it is in finance.

Finance professionals are always trying to look around the corner because being able to see just a little bit ahead is where the money is made. It's the reason that financial technology — FinTech — has been a hot topic for years. And it is the reason why the future of finance is such a hotly discussed subject — and why I wrote this book.

Finance is often at the forefront of technological moves because that's where the money is.

It's why finance professionals often say "follow the money" when it comes to a trade or investable theme.

Interestingly, the big themes of the decade ahead have already started. It's why this book is titled *The Future of Finance is Now*. And I've been talking about the big three levers of finance change for years.

These include **increased access, reduced costs, and easier use.**

The move to democratize financial tools and markets has increased, with people all over the world having more access to payment systems, private equity, and 24-7 banking than ever before.

And there has been a big push to reduce the costs of financial services across the spectrum of activities — from payments to managed accounts. It's why the previously standard notion of "2 and 20," which represented the percentages actively managed funds used to receive on assets under management (AUM), is mostly dead.

Finally, in a world driven by UI/UX metrics, finance has become a sector focused on ease of use, where it was previously a field that sometimes overwhelmed customers with its cumbersome nature.

These three levers of change have impacted FinTech and finance at all levels in recent years — and their impact will continue to impact finance in the decade ahead and beyond. In effect, these levers have been the hallmarks of disruption.

Acknowledgements

This book represents an attempt to share what I have learned in over 15 years of working in finance and in the last three and a half years, since I began digging into the field of FinTech.

But no book is done completely alone. There is editorial, file conversion, design, and project management. And those tasks require a team. Along those lines, I want to thank Prestige Economics and Prestige Professional Publishing staff for making this book a reality. Additionally, I want to especially thank **Nawfal Patel**, who managed the production of *The Future of Finance is Now.*

Most importantly, I want to thank my family for supporting me in my education, career, entrepreneurship, and authorship. I am always most grateful for the support of my loving wife, **Ashley Schenker**, and to my wonderful parents, **Janet and Jeffrey Schenker**. My family supports me in countless ways by providing emotional support and editorial feedback.

Every time I write a book, it's a crazy experience that spills over into my family life, so to them and to everyone else who helped me in this process: Thank you!

Finally, thank you for buying this book. I hope you enjoy *The Future of Finance is Now*!

~ Jason Schenker

THE FUTURE OF FINANCE

Everyone I know gets very excited when they start imagining the future of finance. They see things as being so radically different from the past.

But that isn't true.

The names and technology are changing, but the game is still the same.

In *The Future of Finance is Now*, I present some data and analysis on changing dynamics in the world of finance. And these are couched in the notion that this time is never different.

Big data is no big deal in finance. Financial institutions have always had lots of data to wrangle with. In fact, some of the first writing in recorded history was to keep track of financial records.

This is why **blockchain technology** is not that new either — and it's not because it's over a decade old. It's because blockchain is a kind of accounting software used for record keeping.

Even **quantum computing**, which is a new kind of computing, isn't necessarily different for finance. After all, financial institutions have been trying to find ways to use technological calculations, analysis, and computational processing power to gain an edge in markets ever since the abacus — or at least since the bucket shops of *Reminiscences of a Stock Operator*.

As for **cybersecurity** challenges, those are part of a long-term trend as well. Look, the thieves of the decade ahead may not ride in on a horse, wear a bandana, and have pearl-handled revolvers. And they may not wear a trenchcoat to conceal a Tommy gun. But you can bet your sweet bippy that they're still out to get the goods — even if the main tool of theft today is a computer and an internet connection. Just like in the Wild West or the gangster era, financial institutions will struggle to protect assets in their custody and for which they have fiduciary duty.

Plus, mobsters and terrorists will continue to try and find new digital means of engaging in illicit activities. They may no longer be able to use paper bearer bonds, but **cryptocurrencies** are just a digital equivalent.

On the political side of things, governments will continue to go further into **debt** by spending more than they have. And even communism is likely to make another appearance on the world stage under a new rebranded name of **universal basic income**.

As you can see, a number of new emerging and disruptive technologies and trends impacting the future of finance look similar to ones from time immemorial.

In fact, even the latest trends appear to be well underway and poised to impact finance for decades into the future.

That's why this book is titled *The Future of Finance is Now*.

The Structure of This Book

In order to tackle the most important factors in navigating *The Future of Finance is Now*, I have divided this book into four main sections:

- **Market Trends**
- **Technology Trends**
- **Long-Term Risks**
- **Global Trends**

In the first section, **Market Trends**, I discuss some of the most important recent dynamics in financial markets that are likely to affect the future of finance. These include how technology and finance have often been linked (Chapter 2), the three levers of change for FinTech (Chapter 3), the hunt for yield (Chapter 4), market correlations and interrelated trading (Chapter 5), the push toward alpha capture models over research (Chapter 6), and the phenomenon of hype locusts (Chapter 7).

When I examine **Technology Trends** in the second section of the book, I look at the most critical new and emerging technologies that are likely to impact the future of finance for years and decades to come. These include big data (Chapter 8), automation (Chapter 9), blockchain (Chapter 10), quantum computing (Chapter 11), cybersecurity (Chapter 12), robo-advisors (Chapter 13), and biased AI (Chapter 14).

The third section of this book is dedicated to **Long-Term Risks**. This section includes an examination of U.S. debt and entitlements (Chapter 15), central bank balance sheets and the future quantum state of the economy (Chapter 16), and the rise of universal basic income (Chapter 17).

The fourth and final section of *The Future of Finance is Now* is titled **Global Trends**. This section includes the optimistic look at the beneficial global impacts of FinTech innovations (Chapter 18) as well as the rising importance of ESG and sustainability for companies (Chapter 19) and the importance of trade for the global economy (Chapter 20).

I end *The Future of Finance is Now* with individual, business, and professional recommendations to approach the coming changes in the field of finance.

Okay, that's enough talk about the future.

Let's get to it!

CHAPTER 1

WHY I WROTE THIS BOOK

"Have you done any work on the future of finance?"

It was like one of many questions a booking agent asks when they are trying to feel out a speaker for an event pitch.

But this wasn't a question someone asked me in 1999 when I graduated college. It was a question an agent asked me in 2019.

I'm pretty sure my mouth was wide open in disbelief. In that moment I was glad we were on a phone and not sitting face to face.

The reason I was so surprised, and the reason I wrote this book, is because I had done so much work on the future of finance in the three years leading up to 2019.

After all, I had started writing extensively about the future of finance and FinTech in 2016, when I was working on a FinTech certificate at MIT.

On the lecture circuit, I had also begun incorporating FinTech topics into numerous professional speeches since 2016. In fact, I had a number of these speeches professionally recorded and posted on YouTube, at www.youtube.com/jasonschenker.

And then there was the eponymously titled The Future of Finance course I had created and recorded over two years before this discussion for the initial launch of The Futurist Institute's Certified Futurist and Long-Term Analyst training program.

Plus, by the time we had this call, I had written a number of future technology books that had sections dedicated to the future of finance, including *Jobs for Robots*, *The Promise of Blockchain*, *The Robot and Automation Almanac*, and *Quantum: Computing Nouveau*, as well as my other finance books, *Financial Risk Management Fundamentals* and *A Gentle Introduction to Audit and Due Diligence*.

But this agent didn't seem to know any of this.

So I told him.

Exactly as you just read it.

And then he asked, "So, you are sure you can talk about future of finance then?"

There was no twinge of irony. it was a serious question. Now I was less happy. And my jaw was no longer on the floor. It was clenched.

It was this second ask that really prompted me to write this book.

I know that the notion of using a book as a business card has become commonplace. But I myself sometimes forget that no matter how much research I produce, no matter how many speeches I give, and no matter how many articles or videos I create, it very often does not matter.

If you have not written a book on a certain subject, people won't believe you have any real insight or expertise.

Of course, if you write a book, there still needs to be wisdom or at least kernels of wisdom in it.

As the marketing guru Ryan Holiday once told me, "When you write a book, it has to be good."

Huh.

Who knew?

Well, my friends, I share this advice that came with a $1,000-per-hour price tag so that you now know the biggest secret of books: Write a good one.

Full stop.

But the singular notion of writing a good book is reductive and a gross oversimplification of the reality behind the process

The truth is that "good" is very subjective when it comes to books.

And practical, cutting edge, and innovative is what I am pushing for rather than perennial, pandering, and smarmy.

My belief is that as long as you write a book with value that you can proudly share with the world, you will create a content marketing vehicle to accelerate and propel your professional perception — and career — forward.

Despite my awareness of this and the fact that I became a futurist because of my concern that FinTech could mortally disrupt my then main business, Prestige Economics, I still had someone asking me if I knew about the future of finance.

And so this book was born.

In all truth, this probably should have been my first book on future technology. But it's finally here.

Sometimes when a business grows, you have to go and backfill some of the basics. And while this book has existed in video and online course form for more than two years, it is now finally in print.

So no one may again ask if I know about the future of finance.

Don't get me wrong here.

The future of finance is an amazing and exciting topic.

It is what fundamentally shifted my entire professional career and forced me to pivot from being an economist to becoming a futurist. And FinTech was the primary impetus behind my founding of The Futurist Institute and the creation of the Certified Futurist and Long-Term Analyst™ — FLTA™ — designation.

I was even a FinTech startup founder and executive for a short time in 2016.

Plus, having worked in finance and markets for over 15 years, I have seen a few things. And I've done well at analyzing and predicting them as well — according to Bloomberg, which has ranked me a top forecaster in 43 different categories since 2011.

The future of finance will be exciting and disruptive. And the most interesting part is that most of the changes coming in the decade ahead have already started. In fact, most of them started a few years ago — or longer.

That's why I titled this book *The Future of Finance is Now*, because most of the trends are already in motion.

Finance has always been an industry at the forefront of technology because it provides an edge. And an edge in finance, banking, and trading is where the big money is made.

With that in mind, the future of finance is going to be about market adoption, penetration of emerging technologies into new markets, and complete saturation of certain critical technologies.

But it will also be about ramping up bleeding-edge technologies, like quantum computing, as quickly as possible.

And the future of finance in all its digital and virtual forms will be increasingly about security.

Most of the trends in the future of finance aren't just trends we've seen in the technology field. They are trends that have always existed in finance.

In the chapters ahead, I will discuss some of the most important trends that will rapidly become ubiquitous as well as some that face challenges ahead.

And I will place these trends and technologies in their current and historical context.

After all, this time is never different. That is most certainly true in finance, and it is likely to be true for the future of finance as well.

CHAPTER 2

TECHNOLOGY AND FINANCE

Finance has always been a field at the forefront of technology. It's because that's where the edge is — that's where the money is.

If you are going to allocate technology to industries with high degrees of ROI, finance would be the right place because the business of money is at a position of the fulcrum when it comes to monetizing information.

Of course, I'm not talking about material nonpublic information or anything like that. I'm talking about performing market analysis, identifying data relationships, exploiting correlations, and using technology to build a better mousetrap. Because a little edge can turn into a lot of money when the business of finance is involved.

This is why technologies that we will see in the future of finance are already here. Many of them are accelerating the pace and ease of transactions, reducing costs, and increasing access. I'll discuss these three levers in the next chapter.

Overall, the main takeaway for the future of finance is that any new innovations are likely to be adopted more rapidly by finance than by almost any other industry. Because something that works is likely to generate big financial returns.

Furthermore, even though the trends of the next decade and beyond have already been set in motion for the future of finance, there are likely to be new innovations that pop up. And finance is likely to take up the mantle quickly.

It was a lesson that banks had to learn this cycle.

FinTech was the digital barbarian at the gates, threatening to erode margin. And the banks and traditional financial services firms are finally on board and pushing innovation forward.

This is why many of the big banks started technology accelerators and incubators several years ago. After all, FinTech solutions pose a threat to traditional financial services. And if FinTech was going to eat financial services' lunch, then financial services might as well be pushing FinTech forward. As the saying goes, if you aren't at the table, you're on the menu.

This means that the future of finance is likely to continue to involve traditional financial services firms, using their accelerators and incubators to foster innovation. And it means that there is no going back. The future of finance is FinTech in all of its permutations, and it is driven by three critical levers.

CHAPTER 3

LEVERS OF CHANGE

Financial technology, otherwise known in shorthand as FinTech, is driving innovation and disruption because of three main levers of change.

The first of these is reducing cost. And it's pretty straightforward. FinTech solutions have used technology to reduce costs of financial activities in everything from buying and selling stocks to transferring funds and making as well as receiving payments.

Traditional financial services firms have had to compete with, acquire, or otherwise grow competing solutions in order to remain competitive with some of the lower-cost options that FinTech has brought to the world.

Of course, cost is only one factor that drives consumer decisions. Another, perhaps more critical, factor is user experience. And FinTech solutions generally try to not only reduce costs, but they also strive to improve the customer experience. When provided in concert with lower costs, a FinTech solution has a killer strategic combination.

The third and final lever of FinTech is access. FinTech solutions seek to penetrate new markets and democratise previously limited financial services offerings. A great example of this is private equity crowdfunding. Private equity investments had previously been limited to accredited investors with either high levels of income or assets. Now they are available for everyone.

Digital access to financial services companies has reached some of its greatest penetration for millennials and Generation X. But in the decade ahead, I expect that there will be a big push for older Americans as well as Generation Z to get on online platforms.

The impact for the future of finance is one that will foster a continued move toward a more fully remote, online, and cloud-based nature of investments, financial activities, and the financial services industry overall. As I noted in the last chapter, there is no going back.

This does not mean that all people will eschew transactions done in banks or the in-person advice of a financial advisor. But it does mean that people are looking for low cost, ease of use, and greater access. Those are all easier to provide at scale online with zero marginal cost applications.

Of course, a bifurcation in financial services is likely to emerge, with consumers at the highest end of the market paying a premium, while the average retail investor may struggle to make complicated financial decisions, especially given how low financial literacy is in the United States.

CHAPTER 4

THE HUNT FOR YIELD

One of the biggest challenges of the past few years has been the hunt for yield — the hunt for investment returns. Bond yields are low, Treasury yields are low, real estate prices are up, and equity multiples are high.

So, where are people supposed to invest to generate returns?

This is a particularly gnawing question — especially if you are looking for stable fixed income investments with relatively safe returns. And this isn't just a U.S. phenomenon.

Yields have fallen almost everywhere. In Europe, the ECB still had negative deposit rates when this book when to print — and it is likely to have negative deposit rates for the foreseeable future.

These kinds of challenges could remain in play if the future of finance is one of a persistently low interest rate environment. And if central banks are going to roll out the balance sheets every time there is a downturn in the future, low interest rates could remain ubiquitous.

One of the factors that has been driving yields lower and multiples higher is a greatly reduced number of investible assets. In fact, the number of publicly traded companies has fallen sharply — by almost half — in recent years, as can be seen in Figure 4-1. Furthermore, the number of publicly traded companies is likely to fall further.

This leaves equity investors with fewer assets to chase. And it threatens to further push valuation multiples to unreasonable levels. Part of this dynamic is also being exacerbated by the fact that exchange traded funds (ETFs) have been big buyers of equities. ETFs are a form of passive asset management that I discuss further in Chapter 9. The growth of ETFs can be seen in Figure 9-2.

Figure 4-1: Number of Publicly Traded Companies[1]

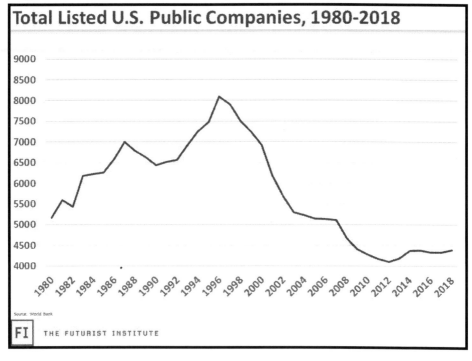

Because the number of ETFs has risen, there are essentially more buyers of the limited supply of equities. And there has been a significantly lower number of IPOs in recent years, keeping the number of total listed public companies at relatively low historical levels. This dynamic can be seen in Figure 4-2.

Continued merger and acquisition (M&A) activity as well as the reduced supply of new companies through IPOs are dual dynamics that threaten to reduce value opportunities for equity investors in the long run.

As with other topics in this book, these dynamics are not new. The train has already left the station for reduced equity investment opportunities.

Figure 4-2: Number of IPOs[2]

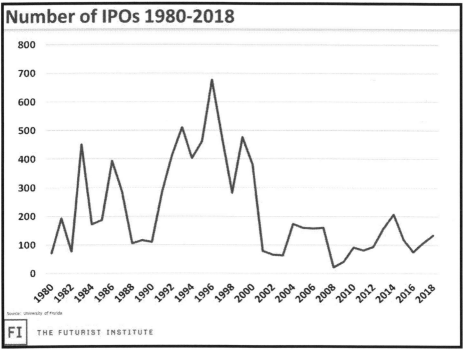

These dynamics are also highly likely to continue into the future of finance. But that's not even the biggest risk in terms of chasing equity investment returns.

A bigger risk for the future of finance — especially in the near term — is that the percentage of IPOs with negative earnings was at 81 percent in 2018 — a figure that equaled the all-time-high percentage of negative earnings IPOs back in 1999, just before the tech bubble burst.[3]

Historically, there has been a rising trend in IPOs with negative earnings, as you can see in Figure 4-3. But the rising trend of negative earnings IPOs during the most recent business cycle has been more drastic than in previous cycles.

Figure 4-3: Number of IPOs With Negative Earnings[4]

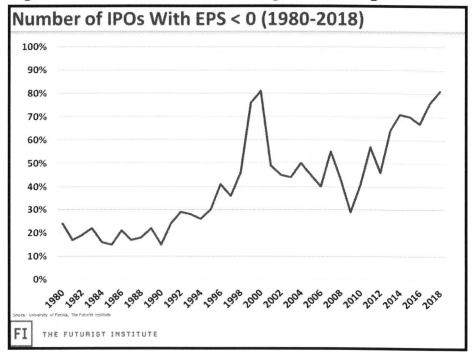

Number of IPOs With EPS < 0 (1980-2018)

Source: University of Florida, The Futurist Institute

FI   THE FUTURIST INSTITUTE

Problematically, this may be a new normal since there are now fewer public companies to invest in. And even if ETFs seek to diversify portfolios, with fewer companies to invest in, that becomes a challenge — and it may be creating additional demand for any kind of assets available, even if they have negative earnings. This may also partially explain why companies that have negative earnings have actually shown greater returns on their IPO days than companies with positive earnings. This dynamic can be seen in Figure 4-4. I mean, how backward is that?

Plus, the margin isn't a small one. In 2018, the average ratio of IPO-day returns for negative earnings companies was double that of companies with positive earnings. This is also true of the average IPO day returns from 1980-2018.[5]

Figure 4-4: Return Ratio of IPOs: Negative / Positive Earnings[6]

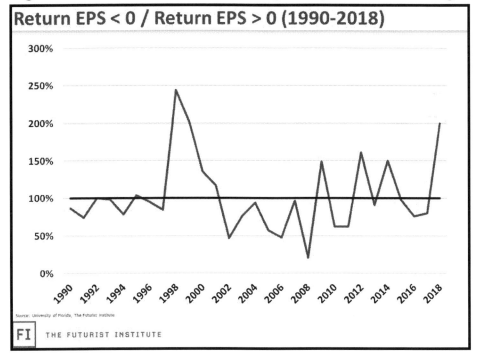

Some analysts and investors typify this dynamic as investing in a "positive return story." In other words, people make investments because the prices have always gone up. This dynamic begins with private funding, where different rounds of funding send valuations of pre-revenue and early-stage companies ever higher. From a seed round to Series A and beyond, all the way until IPO, companies with negative earnings see their valuations rise.

Although the future of finance is likely to continue to see the majority of IPO companies have negative earnings, the current percentage is historically high — and could be in for a correction in the event of a downturn.

For now, however, investors bemoan the lack of investible assets. And the globally coordinated central bank quantitative easing party of the last cycle introduced excess cash and liquidity into markets lacking a potential for returns. The result has been a push into assets that may have inflated valuations. Furthermore, the problems of excess liquidity, lack of investible assets, and FOMO have also crept into the private investing space as well. And some of the deals I have personally seen boggle the mind.

Looking at the future of finance, I expect dynamics in public markets could continue to bleed over into private markets. And while quantitative easing, which I discuss in Chapter 16, was an effective way to stimulate a global economy on the brink of disaster, it has also contributed to excess capital-seeking returns. This has made investments expensive, and it has incentivized some bad behaviors. Historically, there has been a piper to pay when such dynamics continue for too long.

CHAPTER 5

MARKET CORRELATIONS

Market correlations have become increasingly linked in recent years. And they are likely to be more important in the future.

I have often written about market correlations, and it was a critical topic in my book *Commodity Prices 101*. It is also a reality that I have incorporated into my financial market forecasts over the past 15 years. In fact, it is one of the things that has greatly impacted the accuracy of forecasts Prestige Economics has made across asset classes, from foreign exchange rates to energy prices, metals prices, and agricultural commodities.

In short, the future of finance will continue to see cross-market correlated price action. The dollar, gold prices, oil prices, metals prices, and equities will continue to see discernable relationships.

Much of this is due to the financialization, algo trading, and technical trading across markets. As more statistical analyses are performed and models are build, trade decisions will likely continue to reinforce historical relationships that may have been less consistent.

Of course, there will also be some critical monetary policy actions and economic data that may continue to exert an outsized fundamentally justified impact across markets. Quantitative easing across central banks, as I noted in the previous chapter, has had an impact of lifting almost all ships, from equities and commodity prices to hard assets. After all, QE programs are designed to juice aggregate demand. And more global demand drives up prices.

On the fundamental economic side of the equation, I expect to see a continued market-moving importance for the purchasing manager indices (PMIs) as leading reads on capital-intensive manufacturing industries — and GDP overall. In a not-quite 80/20 world, the U.S. ISM Manufacturing Index, Eurozone Manufacturing PMI, and Chinese Caixin Manufacturing PMI offer insight into the overall health of the global economy, despite the minority of global GDP attributable to manufacturing. In short, these are likely to remain critical reports to watch in the future.

In general, I expect that the fundamentals of leading economic indicators and monetary policy will continue to have impacts across financial markets. And that in between those moments of fundamental action — and in response to them — technical trading and correlations across markets will take the reins.

The future of finance for financial market drivers will remain a mix of fundamentals and technicals, while reinforced historical cross-market correlations are likely to become generally tighter over time, effectively removing established and provable arbitrage opportunities across asset classes.

CHAPTER 6

ALPHA CAPTURE

The future of financial market research, like so many other areas of finance, is already here.

And the future is called alpha capture.

In Europe, an update to a regulation known as the Markets in Financial Instruments Directive — MiFID II — came into effect at the beginning of 2018 that required fund managers to unbundle research from the trading and execution components of asset management.

This means that fund managers now have to either pay for research outright themselves, or set up a research payment account with a budget that has been approved by their clients.

In other words, institutional investors and funds now have to get approved funds to buy research. That is a tough ask. It has been catastrophic for firms that produce financial market research for institutional investors. Fortunately, my research firm, Prestige Economics, has always focused on corporate clients.

But the institutional and fund part of the research market was very lucrative, and it allowed individual analysts and small firms working with big funds to do very well.

Of course, those days are over now. And I have seen countless small research firms shutter their operations. I have seen analysts return to large banks and corporations to serve as content marketers rather than remain independent researchers.

But most insidiously, I have seen investment funds that want to compensate researchers by having them engage in something called alpha capture. In short, alpha capture systems involve regulated, licensed researchers inputting trade recommendations directly into a trading platform run by a fund or institutional investor. If the recommendations turn a profit, the analyst gets paid — and the analyst may even be allocated a larger shadow portfolio to manage. But if the recommendations do not make money, the analyst is out.

In some cases, the process on the fund side may be somewhat academic. Maybe someone is reviewing the recommendations carefully and then making their own trade, potentially unlike what the analyst recommended. You know, maybe.

But in other cases, it has seemed to me like shadow portfolio management done at bargain-basement prices. And there may be just an "execute" button on the other end of the trade.

I had two discussions with funds doing alpha capture in 2018. Both times, the potential for regulatory oversight killed the deals.

In one case, a major multibillion-dollar fund in Europe told me I did not need to be regulated. Fortunately, I had two regulators in my office that week for a review of my Texas Registered Investment Advisor, Prestige Asset Management, LLC.

I asked the regulators directly if the fund was correct, and I noted that I suspected the fund was wrong and that this was a regulated activity. After all, making trade recommendations in a system with very specific inputs, dollar amounts, contracts, and so on seemed more like asset management than writing reports about what markets might do. And that would be true even if it didn't look like I was directly inputting actual trades.

Of course, my intuition was correct. This was a regulated activity.

The regulators said so. Explicitly.

When I spoke again with the fund the following week, they again assured me that their U.S. compliance department was certain I did not need to be regulated. So I told them what the regulators said.

And what would "regulation" in that case mean?

Honestly, all it meant was that I had to share my standard and filed disclosure documents that showed I had a clean professional and criminal background.

And I had to share my maximum fees, although the minimum was set at zero and dependent on performance.

In the end, the fund refused to sign forms that were just a disclosure for their legal benefit. It appeared as if they did not want an analyst to participate that was regulated.

And yet before approving me for their platform, they required me to have a CRD number with FINRA, the U.S. regulator.

In other words, they wanted to ensure I was regulated. But they did not want to sign anything confirming I was regulated or that the activities I was engaging in for the fund were regulated.

This means that they wanted me to be regulated. But they did not want the regulatory oversight to extend to their platform or activities.

I had a similar situation evolve with a second fund.

So, why would you want someone to be regulated if you would then be unwilling to sign something confirming your maximum potential compensation for them — and that you had received legal and regulatory disclosures for your benefit?

I have my theories.

And I am sure you might have your own now too.

The scary thing is that I know there are a large number of analysts that contribute to these alpha capture systems.

And if this is the regulatory policy de rigueur — confirm you are regulated for me, but I won't sign your legally required paperwork from the regulator — then many of those analysts could eventually find themselves in regulatory hot water.

It may also mean that since funds do not want regulatory oversight to extend over into their fund that they may be actively trying to capture trades from those with outsized positive returns.

I should also note that these kinds of alpha capture funds may want you to sign a disclaimer that your trade recommendations are all legal and based on public information only. But with hundreds of analysts contributing to these platforms and regulatory oversight limited from piercing such funds, I wonder if the goal is to completely obfuscate any trade recommendations informed by material nonpublic information.

Is it all for plausible deniability?

Or is it to keep regulators away from an intentional mix of both modestly positive and very outsized trades? In other words, is it to keep trades mixed together like a goulash, in which you can clearly taste the paprika but can never actually identify exactly where it is?

I know not.

But I wonder.

And as research gets further decoupled from trading and execution at institutional investors in the United States and elsewhere, we could see a further proliferation of alpha capture systems. Some of these may be above board, and some may not.

In either case, independent research is likely to be decimated further. And analysts may have to make Faustian deals with funds using less-than-kosher alpha capture systems to stay afloat.

This is very likely the future of financial market research for those companies that focus on institutional investors and funds.

Fortunately, that's not the focus of my firm,

I hope I'm wrong about all of this.

But I doubt it.

CHAPTER 7

HYPE LOCUSTS

Now we need to have a really unpleasant conversation.

About hype locusts.

This is an ever-increasing and all-too-common phenomenon where a technology topic becomes in vogue, and the media, social media, and then broader society extrapolate the emergence of an emerging new technology to assume it will instantly reach scale to solve some major economic or societal global problem.

The assumption is that these problems are effectively solved the very second any kind of technology is invented. And this causes a swarm of mindless attraction. Hence the term *hype locusts*.

As the hype locusts swarm, they can impact financial markets and private company funding rounds and valuations, and they can even impact political discourse and drive policy to impractical places.

But there is immense danger in the foregone overextended teleological assumptions about a technology as deus ex machina that can make resolving a major fundamental global problem into a simple fait accompli.

Fortunately, this is easy to identify using Google Trends data. But unfortunately, this has been occurring across fields.

It is something that can be seen in the hype around electric vehicles, which is a topic I discussed in my book *The Future of Energy*.

And it is also something that happened with Bitcoin in 2017.

The Hype Correlation

In December 2017, as the price of Bitcoin surged, I saw a sign on the side of the road near my house that said "Bitcoin ATM." It was next to a sign for "We buy houses." As the kids say, "Seems legit."

But only ironically.

In fact, the number of scams around Bitcoin and ICOs became a massive problem. In April 2018, the Texas State Securities Board published a scathing report about cryptocurrency scams.[1]

The price surge in Bitcoin pulled in massive interest around ICOs and blockchain. The volume surged on price, as you can see in Figure 7-1, but so did the question on Google, "What is Bitcoin?" You can see the spike in Google searches in Figure 7-2.

Figure 7-1: The Price of Bitcoin[2]

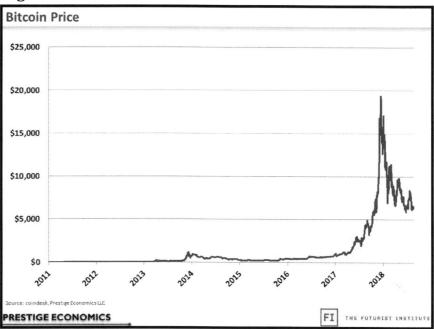

Figure 7-2: Google Trends "What is Bitcoin?"[3]

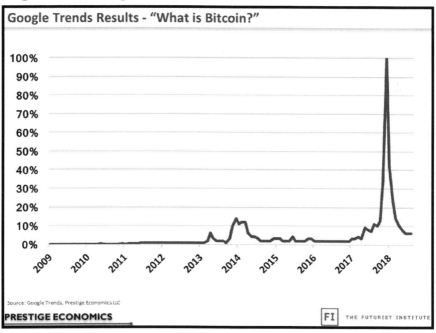

These Google searches indicate the attraction to Bitcoin as an investment by people who did not even know the first thing about it. And dumb money followed lucky money.

And for those companies looking to pull a fast one and rebrand as a blockchain entity, the regulators were watching them too.

In December 2017, near the height of the Bitcoin price bubble, an iced tea company, Long Island Iced Tea Corp., announced a name change to Long Blockchain Corp. This name change caused the company's price to spike from around $2 per share to almost $7 per share. An investigation into the company was subsequently launched, and the price of the company came crashing down to around $0.34 per share as of 1 August 2018.[4]

The Nasdaq also delisted the company, removing it from its public equity exchange, and the U.S. Securities and Exchange Commission subpoenaed the organization on 10 July 2018. This does not seem to bode well for its management, and it should serve as a cautionary tale about trying to ride a bubble, the power of regulators, and the hype around blockchain.

Is Quantum Locust-Ready?

Quantum computing is also at risk of being exposed to the same potential pressures of hype locusts as blockchain.

For now, there are zero publicly traded companies in the quantum computing space. And yet, beginning in September 2018, there was at least one exchange-traded fund (ETF) purporting to be a quantum ETF.

But the problem is that without any purely publicly traded quantum companies, this could be more of a hype-ready name and label, rather than a basket of quantum investments.

Of course, that doesn't mean such an ETF isn't investing in companies working on quantum. In fact, that's one of its core claims. And it also doesn't mean the ETF won't do well. After all, it may do well if the companies it invests in do well.

But it does mean that there aren't publicly traded quantum companies in the composition of the quantum ETF. It's an ETF for an industry that doesn't yet exist. And it hints at the potential risks ahead for a hype bubble around quantum.

At the moment, real money is coming into quantum.

And the hype locusts are waiting. Their frenzy is likely to materialize at some point in the not-too-distant future. It may even come on the back of the reductively bullish notion of a megatrend, making it essentially an anointed "sure thing" investment to those exposed to the investment-return-story notions of our current hype-locust-ridden financial Zeitgeist.

But this time is never different. And by any other name, these swarms of hype locusts create investment bubbles.

And bubbles burst.

It happened to the tulips, it happened to tech in 2001, it happened to Bitcoin in 2018, and it will also continue to happen in the future of finance.

The Outlook? Bubbles With a Swarm of Hype Locusts

Looking ahead at the future of finance and hype locusts, I expect more hype bubbles that are inspired by content marketing that turns organically or inorganically viral, resulting in a social media maelstrom of hype, which eventually turns into real media coverage — and investor dollars.

This is the dream of every underfunded startup that squeezes its last few dollars raised into marketing for the next round rather than investing funds into a prototype of their actual product.

Since the algos follow the data to follow the money, the money often follows the locusts.

It's not that the world has changed completely. It's rather that the Blue Horseshoe hotline is now in the hands of growth hackers. And the algos that take their cues from social media and earned coverage are just waiting to play the bigger fools.

The mediums are digital as opposed to analog, but the impact is the same as it always was. And the outcome for this kind of investing is likely to end as it has for so many in the past: in tears.

I expect this kind of phenomenon to continue in the decade ahead as the overdemocratization of media and content leads to further false positives in the investing world. It also means that company social media footprints are poised to become increasingly critical parts of marketing strategies — and potentially market valuations.

CHAPTER 8

BIG DATA

A Google executive speaking at a conference in Houston in October 2018 noted that the volume of data collected between 2016 and 2018 was greater than the amount of data created and collected in all previous human history.[1]

Businesses live and breathe data. They are expecting to find their next customers, cut costs, choose their next initiatives, and optimize their activities by analyzing data. But the risk of computational data analysis paralysis is real if the data sets are too unwieldy for the computational powers at our disposal.

If the only solution to processing more data is *more* processors — rather than *better* processors — then the cost to analyze data is going to be an issue that increases with the volume of data. In other words, the cost to buy more processors to get the job done could also go parabolic. And that is becoming a real risk.

In a data-rich field like finance, this could become a critical issue in the decade ahead.

The End of Moore's Law

Part of the reason for the massive shift and increase in data volumes has been a massive decline in the cost of data processing and data storage hardware. But that may be coming to end — especially for processing power costs.

This is because computational powers are facing some potential limitations. In fact, many people working in technology will speak about a big near-term risk, and that's the limit of something called Moore's Law, which is named after Intel founder Gordon Moore. It is the notion that computational powers can be doubled while the costs are halved.[2]

This has made increasing computer processing power technology both more powerful and cheaper. A graphical depiction of the development of computer processing power along the lines of Moore's Law is depicted in Figure 8-1.

But Moore's Law is breaking down.[3] The computational increases with lower costs just aren't happening anymore.

In truth, the only solution now is more processors versus better processors. And this is a really big problem as the amount of data being created accelerates. After all, if you want to be able to analyze data you collect, you need processors that can handle the amount of data you are collecting.

This is going to become more of a challenge as the amount of data we collect and store continues to rise parabolically, especially in an *internet of things* — or IoT — world.

Currently, we have an internet of computers, tablets, and cell phones. Those are the primary devices that have internet connectivity and through which data can be collected and tasks enacted.

But the drop in sensor costs and a desire for increased consumer convenience is going to usher in an era called the internet of things, when many things are connected to the internet, not just your computer, tablet, or phone. These could include your car, refrigerator, and office supply closet.

Each of these devices will interact, take actions, and generate data. When all devices are connected to the internet, the amount of additional, minable, analyzable data will be mind blowing.

Figure 8-1: Moore's Law[4]

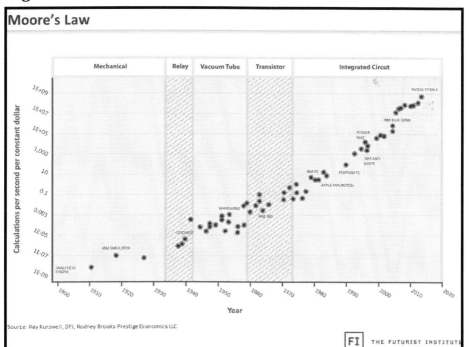

Current levels of existing data collection and analysis will likely pale in comparison to future IoT data. And some of that IoT data is likely to be used in financial services , banking, and insurance.

Now, when it comes to processing power, without a step change from technology like quantum computing, the only strategy available would be buying more processors rather than making significantly cheaper or better processors. This is talked about in technology circles as a kind of "brute force" solution.[5] Technology experts, scientists, and futurists use this term because buying more processors isn't inventive.

It's a problem solved by money rather than scientific innovation. It's just throwing more processors at the problem rather than pushing for a step change in computational processing power.

Data Challenges Are Different
IoT devices will offer greater access to data in the future than in the present. And hardware may offer the processing power to make analysis more — or less — expensive, depending on whether universal quantum computing gets to commercialization quickly.

But the situation for data analysis is different.

You can throw as much money at the hardware as you like, but that isn't the biggest challenge when it comes to data analysis. Throwing more money and processing at significantly higher volumes of data just isn't enough. It won't help make sure the analysis is good. It won't solve the actual biggest data challenges.

These are some of the reasons that quantum computing, which I discuss in Chapter 11, will become a critical technology as the sheer volume of data we are collecting rises.

In finance circles, the amount of publicly available data is already mind blowing. After all, graphs and charts can be taken from the daily level to the hourly level, the minute level, and even the tic level. In order to develop an edge in trading, you need to be a bit ahead of everyone else.

It's a critical reason why so many high-frequency trading firms in New York are located in Manhattan, so that they can be closest to fiber optic cables that let them execute their trades milliseconds sooner than other firms.[6]

And this kind of push for the slimmest of edges, leveraging all of the available data and the swiftest execution, will become more critical in the future — especially since trading has become, and will further become, automated.

Data Goes on the Balance Sheet

There is one other final point that needs to be considered about the relationship between data and finance. Some companies currently have line items on their balance sheets for data. The evaluation and consideration of data as a balance sheet asset is likely to increase in the years ahead. This means that data isn't just something that traders will need to have a better handle on. It means that as a resource, more data will have a positive impact on company valuations.

CHAPTER 9

AUTOMATION

Yes, the robots are coming for low-skill, low-income, and low-education jobs. But, they are coming for other jobs too. I learned several years ago that they are coming for mine. And if you work in finance, they may be coming for your job too.

You Might Not Hear the Robots Coming

The first time I heard the word *FinTech*, I was at the Atlanta Federal Reserve Bank's Financial Markets Conference on Amelia Island in May 2016. At this annual meeting, which I have attended nine times, about 150 of the world's top economists are invited to join regional Fed bank presidents, government regulators, academics, and often the Chairman of the Federal Reserve to discuss the hottest economic, monetary policy, and fiscal policy issues of the day.

Against a backdrop of this prestigious conference, a Fed reporter I have known for years and I skipped out of some sessions to enjoy the beautiful early May Florida weather.

My friend was with another reporter whose specialty was FinTech. At the time, I had not yet heard of FinTech. So I asked naively, "What's that?" The reporter told me FinTech was "like Bitcoin and stuff like that." I knew Bitcoin was a digital currency, so that was that.

I didn't think too much of this conversation until several months later, when I tried to hire a salesperson for Prestige Economics. I had difficulty finding candidates.

Highly qualified people were exiting the space in droves. And I didn't know why.

Finally, one senior salesperson told me that everyone was getting out of financial market research because of FinTech. Essentially, robots were disrupting the research business. After being told that FinTech was disrupting my own business, I decided to learn as much as possible about it by taking a FinTech course at MIT. In short, the robots had been coming for me, and I hadn't even known it.

FinTech: Robocalypse Comes to Finance

FinTech is a buzzword for financial technology, which represents a host of businesses that are designed to disrupt (and eat the lunch of) traditional financial institutions. FinTech companies generally reduce costs, reduce complexity, or increase ease of use for transactions that had previously been the domain of banks.

FinTech is affecting financial services, and awareness has been spreading.

Asset management has long been dominated by computers, statistical analysis, and programming. And FinTech has been disrupting asset management — often with passive trading strategies. Some of these strategies are known as robo-advising, due to their automated (i.e., robot-like) nature. And the result? Asset managers are losing their jobs, and the disruption potential for asset management is very high (Figure 9-1).

In the movie *Wall Street*, Gordon Gekko asks Bud Fox, "Ever wonder why fund managers can't beat the S&P 500?" Well, with the advent of exchange traded funds (ETFs), fund managers and retail investors can just buy the S&P (and other indices), which is what they have done. A number of these ETFs are very liquid.

Figure 9-1: Impact of FinTech on Financial Advice[1]

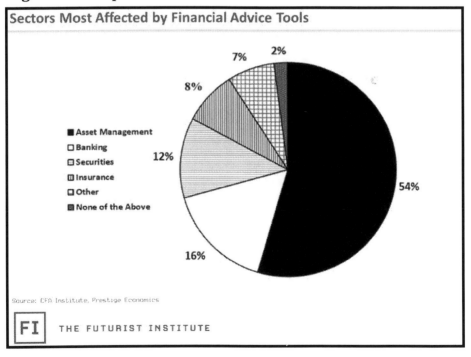

Passive asset management techniques and robo-advising are often easier and cheaper to administer than active asset management. These strategies can be implemented at significantly lower costs than active asset management strategies because they no longer require human asset managers. Plus, there is an economy of scale, when computer programs do all the strategy work, analysis, and planning as well as all of the buying and selling of securities.

And passive asset management has also been adopted by finance and trading because these fields have historically embraced technology, with many firms using black box, algorithmic, and technical trading strategies for many years.

Figure 9-2: Number of ETFs[2]

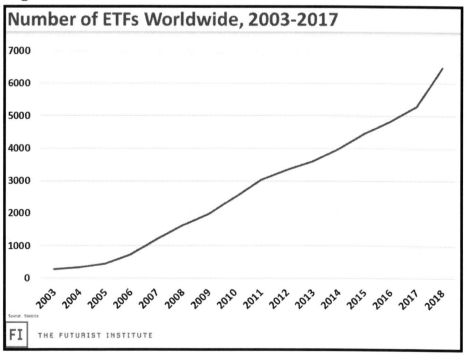

Expensive items (like market research) would also no longer be part of the budget since decisions are made by computers. After all, trading computer programs do not read words. But they really like lines — especially lines above (or below) which the price of a traded security has consistently stayed for a long time.

Technical trading has become more important, so analysts have been trying to add value by knowing what lines and supports matter most for the computers in different markets. This is why there has been a significant uptick in the number of financial professionals pursuing the Chartered Market Technician® — or CMT® — designation. I completed the CMT® in 2016, and it focuses exclusively on these kinds of technical trading dynamics. Essentially, you are looking for the computers in the market. I incorporated these technical trading dynamics into my forecasting long ago, which is why I have long expected that these kinds of trading dynamics will become increasingly important as passive asset management and robo-advising continue to grow.

In Texas, Everyone Knows
When I first started working on the book *Jobs for Robots* in 2016, I thought I was one of the few people concerned with the issues of automation, robots, and the future of work. And this is a sentiment I have seen held by executives and industry groups to whom I have spoken in the past few years. But the truth is, everyone has been thinking about this — and everyone knows. Not just me. Not just CEOs. Everyone.

I am a Texan who lives and works in Austin. And everyone in Texas knows that Austin is an important technology hub.

But what most people don't know is that the topic of the future of work has already permeated deep into the heart of Texas. An example of this can be seen in the ad in Figure 9-3.

I often ask groups where they think this poster was hanging in July 2016. I tell them that the ad was hanging in a Texas airport, which it was. And I ask them where they believe the subjects of robo-advising, FinTech, automation, robots, and AI are hot in Texas. I ask them to tell me where they think this poster was hung to resonate with the local population in July 2016.

Groups guess Austin, Dallas, and Houston. But they never guess where it really was: Amarillo.

The implication is clear: Automation is coming to finance in a big way!

Everyone in Texas already knows. Now you do too.

Figure 9-3: Jobs for Robots in Texas

CHAPTER 10

BLOCKCHAIN

Despite its existence for almost a decade, when people talk about the future of finance, blockchain is often at the top of the list. The interest in blockchain was fueled greatly by the cryptocurrency bubble in late 2017, which has traders asking, "When moon? When Lambo?"

This mantra can be explained as embodying two questions:
- *When will the value of my cryptocurrency go to the moon?*
- *When can I buy a Lamborghini with my modest investment?*

But blockchain is about a lot more than Lambos! And there is a lot of misunderstanding and confusion that surrounds the topic.

In short, blockchain is like a combustion engine. In the way that a combustion engine can be used in any number of different vehicles, blockchain technology can be as well.

Blockchain is, in effect, a kind of database with specialized permissions and data sharing that has significant value for corporations and society.

Like many other trends and technologies in this book, blockchain has been around for some time. After all, the first official Bitcoin transaction that was implemented using blockchain technology occurred in January 2009. As I've noted many times, this time is never different — especially not in finance!

Databases and recordkeeping have been around for millennia. In fact, some of the first recorded writings are based on transactional records. So it should be no surprise that advances in technology that advance transactional recordkeeping would be important — or that they would be continually improving.

Plus, the moons and the Lambos only showed up in late 2017, and companies only began to actually look at blockchain in terms of deployment and physical use cases in 2018 and 2019. This means that for the future of finance, considering the deployment and use of blockchain as a technology — and cryptocurrencies for digital payment purposes — will be an evolving process in the decades ahead.

It is also not likely to be a straight line from now to all crypto. This is because cryptocurrency blockchain technology was originally designed to circumvent traditional financial systems and structures as well as AML/KYC financial regulations.

Best in a Distributed Network
There are a few caveats about a blockchain that help elucidate its usefulness and purpose. The first of these is that blockchain works best in a distributed network.

In Figure 10-1, you can see what a distributed network looks like. It's when you have a number of different parties engaging in transactions and there is no central organization to the nature of these transactions. This is like what happens with regionalized businesses or what might happen with how members of a family might spend their income. You have independence of actions and no natural central repository for all records.

Of course, a set of records can be created and shared with a distributed network for any kind of transaction. But this has historically proved clunky.

Anyone who's ever been cc'd on an email chain for a major project knows how difficult it can be to keep track of every update. Plus, sometimes the wrong files are updated, and this can lead to errors.

Figure 10-1: Distributed Network

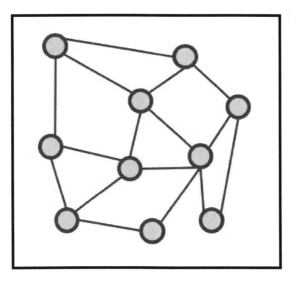

When I worked in management consulting at McKinsey between 2007 and 2009, this was referred to as version control. And it was a major risk in almost any project or client engagement. Sometimes people would update the wrong file, and then important documents were at risk of being incomplete or overwritten. And they would subsequently necessitate complicated reconciliation and review.

This is also a problem with accounting, which is why for audits, tracking financial documents is critical. For auditors, ensuring a consistency of the data through proper sampling and testing is designed to reveal the kinds of problems that stem from improperly kept records — records that are more prone to errors in distributed networks.

Of course, fixing the risks of record keeping in a distributed network is something that cloud computing was designed to do.

In cloud computing technology, people in different locations can edit documents that are updated in a shared location. But those documents are usually kept in a centralized location, and they do not always keep an easy-to-track record of who updated what and when. In some ways, this makes cloud computing like a centralized network, as in Figure 10-2, where all permissions and data are kept in one place. It also means that the network can be vulnerable to a central point of failure.

And a central point of failure risk is one in which records are at risk because they are kept in one place — like Dropbox or Google Drive.

After all, if Dropbox or Google Drive stop working due to a technology problem, it also means that you may not be able to access your documents. And your system of documentation and record keeping will fail through no fault of your own, at least temporarily.

Blockchain technology is different than cloud computing because it is explicitly designed to allow people within a distributed system to receive updated, permanent ledgers of completed transactions. It is designed to reduce central point of failure risk.

But then there is the whole cryptocurrency piece — and those darn Lambos! But before we talk about crypto, let me just reiterate that blockchain is the technology engine that powers Bitcoin and other cryptocurrencies in a permanent distributed ledger. But blockchain can power many things.

Figure 10-2: Centralized Network

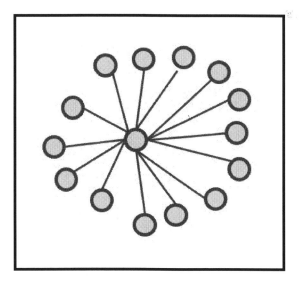

Die Hard Crypto

Maybe it is because the name Satoshi Nakamoto is fake and it sounds Japanese. Maybe it's because people use crypto for faceless, nameless, anonymous transactions that it evokes another fake Japanese-sounding name for me: Nakatomi Plaza.

This isn't a real place either.

It's where the first *Die Hard* film takes place — where the villain of the movie, thief-cum-terrorist Hans Gruber, played by Alan Rickman, is trying to steal bearer bonds.

And what are bearer bonds?

Well, that's the really interesting part: Bearer bonds are a kind of bond that no longer exists. They are called bearer bonds because they are owned by the person who bears them.

If you have them in your possession, you own them. If you don't have them in your possession, you don't own them.

You can see a U.S. bearer bond in Figure 10-3.

While bearer bonds were first issued in the United States in the second half of the 19th century, they stopped being issued in 1982.[1] Today, they are all but extinct.

The reason?

Anti-money laundering.

Anti-money laundering, or AML, as most finance people know it, is the set of legal initiatives taken by governments and financial institutions to prevent and hinder terrorists, criminals, and other bad actors from being able to engage in actions by making it difficult to transfer, hide, and otherwise use money.

And how was it that these bonds were so convenient for money laundering? Well, since these bonds were owned by the person who held them (i.e., the bearer), and there was no trading account or electronic or paper record required to redeem them, they could be bought, sold, and traded in an untraceable manner.

Figure 10-3: U.S. Government Bearer Bond[2]

This means that bearer bonds can be used for money laundering and all kinds of other nefarious things. It's the reason the villain in the *Die Hard* movie wanted to get them, because they could not be traced, and they could be used for illegal activities.

Without any record keeping, bearer bonds could be easily used in illegal commerce without concern of detection because you wouldn't need to go into a Chase Bank branch or log into your Fidelity trading account to buy and sell them. You would, quite literally, take a suitcase of money and hand it to a fellow mobster or terrorist who would, in turn, give you the bearer bond.

So why do bearer bonds make me think of the interplay between Bitcoin and *Die Hard*?

That's simple.

Bitcoin and other cryptocurrencies can be used namelessly. Facelessly. Anonymously. They are digital bearer bonds.

And like physical bearer bonds before them, these digital bearer bonds are only owned by people who have the digital key. And they can be used for nefarious purposes.

But while bearer bonds are all but extinct because of AML initiatives, regulation has seriously lagged behind crypto. Bitcoin and cryptocurrencies are ascending, and they have not been outlawed in most countries despite their ease of use to violate AML laws.

The irony of cryptocurrencies, of course, is that the idea of nongovernment currency started as a vision of Austrian economists and free market libertarians.

Yet while these same libertarians may praise the freedom of operating a currency outside of government, if their Bitcoin gets stolen, the police and the FBI will surely be their first phone call as a recourse of action.

But it may all be for naught. After all, even though transactions on the ledger are permanent, they are difficult to track down because of the built-in anonymity of cryptocurrencies. And even if improving forensics could help trace ill-gotten crypto leveraging the records of a permanent ledger, stopping transactions as they happen would still be quite impossible.

So, as paragons of economic theory dream of the freedom crypto brings, the Hans Grubers of the world — including ISIS, anarchists, political subversives, organized criminals, and the rest of the digital underworld — rejoice in the ignorance and naiveté of those dreams.

Policymakers Know

Fortunately, policymakers and governments have figured out the potential problems with cryptocurrencies, as an anonymous means for bad actors to circumvent regulated structures.

Christine Lagarde, the head of the International Monetary Fund, spoke on the topic of cryptocurrencies at a conference titled Terrorism Financing: The Other War Against Al-Qaida and Daesh.

At that event on 26 April 2018, Lagarde noted:

> **[FinTech] can be used to promote and fund terrorism through the anonymity of crypto-assets.** But leveraged effectively, fintech can also be a powerful tool to fight terrorism and its financing.[3]

The Bank of International Settlements, which is considered the central bank of central banks, noted in June 2018:

> They lack a legal entity or person that can be brought into the regulatory perimeter. **Cryptocurrencies live in their own digital, nationless realm and can largely function in isolation from existing institutional environments or other infrastructure.** Their legal domicile — to the extent they have one — might be offshore, or impossible to establish. As a result, they can be regulated only indirectly.[4]

The big takeaway is that cryptocurrencies exist outside of legal frameworks, and their anonymity facilitates terrorism funding.

More recently, Facebook announced its intent to create a cryptocurrency known as Libra. This was a hot topic for Jay Powell, Chairman of the U.S. Federal Reserve, in his semiannual testimony before Congress in July 2019.[5]

For now, the cryptocurrency story has yet to fully play out. There are still many questions that need to be answered for regulators to give approval. And there is no guarantee that their complete approval will ever come.

Furthermore, any cryptocurrencies that attempt to circumvent or subvert current, dominant, global finance structures may find themselves on the wrong side of regulation for a long time to come.

Assessing the Future Potential of Blockchain

The potential impact of blockchain is bigger than most people can imagine but not nearly as great as some believe. And while many people think blockchain is just crypto, that's only the tip of the iceberg. This was the cornerstone of a talk I gave at SXSW in March 2017.

The impact on corporate supply chains — on logistics, transport, and freight — is going to be massive. And there are a number of other industries, like finance and agriculture, where a chain of custody of ownership and good record keeping is likely to provide a significant value proposition for blockchain.

After all, blockchain allows for a permanent distributed ledger, and if used in a private, commercial endeavor, it could provide instant transparency of origin, content, and custody, which is often required from a regulatory framework for conflict minerals, chemical content, or trade. And this kind of transparency can all have significant value from a public health and safety standpoint, as is the case with agricultural products and food safety.

The potential for blockchain to add economic value in many different industries and corporate fields is massive. But it isn't equal across industries. The biggest value proposition is where there are supply chains and risks to mitigate, as well as health and safety issues.

Assets in Transition See Greatest Use Case

The value proposition in using blockchains for record keeping on long-lived assets is lower than for assets that move. This is true whether we are talking about financial assets that frequently move between investments, markets, and parties — or assets that physically move or are in flux. This impacts The Futurist Institute's assessment for blockchain use potential in Figure 10-4.

In addition to movement factors driving the use case and value proposition for blockchain, there are limitations on blockchain's potential uses in some industries due to incumbent regulatory requirements and dominant legal frameworks — especially in the United States. This is why healthcare, property, and government data uses for blockchain may prove more limited.

Figure 10-4: Assessment of Blockchain Potential

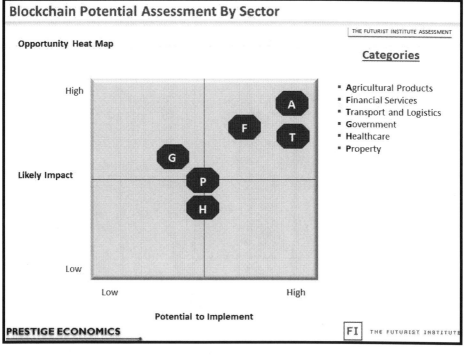

It also explains why there is potential for blockchain use in agricultural products, transport and logistics, and financial services.

The Futurist Institute's Financial Services Assessment

As the Chairman of The Futurist Institute, I directed an analysis and study of corporate and commercial opportunities in blockchain across industries. The overview is in Figure 10-4. Additionally, in Figure 10-5, you can see The Futurist Institute's assessment of the potential uses of blockchain in financial services. The areas where we see the most potential and greatest likelihood for blockchain use overall are in the areas of trade finance and B2B payments.

Figure 10-5: Financial Services Blockchain Assessment

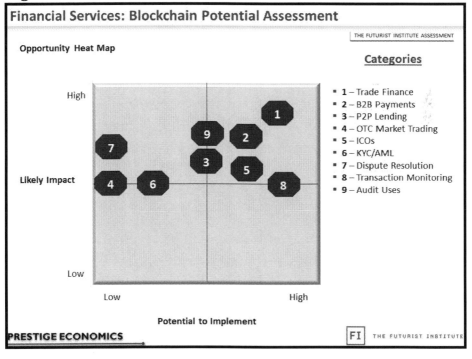

This reflects a focus on corporate transactions as being of both the highest value and greatest importance from financial record keeping and commercial standpoints. In other words, using blockchains in these areas is likely to bring significant value to large entities — and the economy overall.

From an oversight and regulatory standpoint, I expect a high potential for blockchain implementation in transaction monitoring. This is not, however, something I would identify as a high-value activity for the economy. After all, it is a layer of oversight and regulation but not necessarily something that would likely contribute to the operational ROI of a business. The potential to reduce fraud, however, could generate value.

Areas with a low potential in financial services, in our estimation, are in more complicated financial markets like over-the-counter (OTC) trading. In many cases, annotating and tracking complicated financial structures could prove cumbersome. After all, financial exchanges are very sophisticated, and if these OTC transactions are too complicated for exchanges, it seems likely that they may require a lot of hand cranking, in which case a blockchain may not prove useful. And since these are relatively rare, it may not be very impactful for the financial services industry or the economy overall.

Blockchain is likely to be used in a number of other areas as well. But one topic that might stand out is our assessment of the use of blockchain for ICOs. Although blockchain has been inherently tied to cryptocurrencies as the technology that powers them, the regulatory risk for initial coin offerings presents challenges.

Often described as pre-revenue IPOs, ICOs could come under more regulatory oversight, hampering or killing them — and the use of blockchain in their execution. This will depend very much on the future regulatory structure, which is still evolving.

If ICOs can demonstrate an adherence to and compliance with securities laws and oversight, then they may become accepted in the decades ahead. For now, hedge funds and other risk-seeking investors may continue to seek out cryptocurrencies in the hunt for yield. But whether cryptocurrencies of various stripes have a staying power as an investment class remains to be seen.

And the outlook for crypto is still mixed, even if the outlook for blockchain use in record keeping is much more promising.

In some ways, blockchain is a technology that seems custom made for industries with high transaction volumes as well as tracking, regulatory, and safety requirements. This includes finance, transport and logistics, and agriculture. And while blockchain technology is likely to move forward, cryptocurrencies, and Bitcoin in particular, face significant risks.

For now, blockchain technology offers the hope and promise of distributed information and knowledge that can reduce costs, add economic value, and prevent a Library of Alexandria-level loss of information and institutional knowledge for corporate, governmental, and private entities. These have been some of the greatest potential contributions that blockchain is likely to make in the years ahead — and they were the focus of my book *The Promise of Blockchain*.

And yet blockchain is still seen as hype. It is still seen as Lambos.

It has been tied to the biggest investment bubble in the history of the world. And when it is used for unregulated cryptocurrency transactions, it could be the fire that threatens to destroy civilization by allowing for terrorists, anarchists, mobsters, and politically subversive entities to thrive.

That is why I see so much promise for blockchain as an emerging disruptive technology. And why I see both the hope and the hype will continue in the future of finance. In the end, regulation and compliance will be key drivers of future adoption of crypto by finance in the United States and other advanced economies.

CHAPTER 11

QUANTUM COMPUTING

Quantum computing is a technology that will allow for a computational step change.

Essentially all computers we use today operate on a binary computational model — 1s and 0s, like the digital chain image on the cover of my book *The Promise of Blockchain*. The use of 1 or 0 in computation is called a bit, the portmanteau for a binary digit.

But quantum computing is not just 1s and 0s, which are often seen as allegories for a bit that is either "on" and "off." In a quantum computing world, there are bits with other states of being between 1 and 0, called *qubits*, whereby they can be either on, off, or both on and off at the same time.

As for the impact of quantum computing, adding additional states of being to the computational process may not sound like much, but the exponential impact for computing power is likely to be absolutely massive, which is why it could be important for the future of finance as well as for blockchain and other technologies.

Quantum computing could prove to be a critical technological step change that will materially impact business, science, communications, cybersecurity, and national security. But there are limitations, risks, and challenges ahead for quantum computing to achieve a true level of commercialization viability.

While some industries will benefit from specific new and emerging technologies, quantum computing has the potential to impact a wide range of industries in a general purpose fashion — as has occurred with other kinds of computers.

Like with classical, non-quantum computers, some industries will benefit disproportionately from the use of, and leverage provided by, more advanced computational power. The industries most likely to benefit are those that have massive amounts of data that need to be analyzed.

Finance will likely be one of those fields that benefits early and asymmetrically from the ability to use quantum computers to analyze financial markets. This is why quantum computing appears in this book on the future of finance.

But quantum requires both a software and a hardware change. In fact, right now, one of the biggest physical challenge to true quantum computing is temperature, because a true quantum computer needs to operate at near absolute zero temperatures.

That means big physical and material science challenges lie ahead for quantum.

Of course, this doesn't mean that you will someday have a giant quantum computer in your house that is being cooled to near absolute zero temperatures.

But it could mean that you are leveraging that kind of tech in the cloud, as a processor that you access on demand, in a quantum as a service (QaaS) platform framework. This would be like many other kinds of cloud-based technologies and applications.

Of course, there is also the potential that you could have on-site room temperature coprocessors with the emulated quantum computer technology that Brian La Cour has been working on. And the photonic quantum computer that Jeremy O'Brien is working on. But those will still be different from true quantum computing.

For true quantum. we will likely get there because we have to. And in the highest-value use cases, it's critical to remember that quantum is likely to be not just useful — but also necessary. After all, data is being created at a breakneck pace. And as that data collection increases, more analytics and a better way to break down the meaning of the numbers will be critical.

Changes in data, including creation and collection of more data and so-called Big Data, as well as the need for predictive analytics and artificial intelligence, will be supportive of the application of quantum technologies. And in fact, they may necessitate quantum. This means that quantum computing is likely in the very near future to be not just nice to have, but it could become a conditio sine qua non.

It could in that respect be a core requirement for more expansive and extensive data analysis, especially to solve what I call corporate NP (non-deterministic polynomial time) problems of optimization, efficiency, and outlier identification. And it could help us push toward scientific and medical insights that are just too difficult to see with panel data that stretches the limits of current computational and statistical processing powers.

Of course, we will need to ask the right questions. And we will need to follow a proven and structured data analysis process. If we can do that right, however, quantum could be a gold mine for data research, scientific research, and society at large.

It would also be invaluable for the future of finance.

But quantum is not without its risks for the world. Quantum could present catastrophic risks for blockchain technology, cryptocurrencies, and all kinds of encryption technology.

The highest-potential use case for quantum computing is widely expected to be in breaking encryptions and rendering all current forms of cybersecurity useless. And that means we need to be ready for these widely anticipated threats. But aside from the cybersecurity risks that may impact all businesses, governments, and individuals, most people may not directly notice the changes that quantum computing brings.

In fact, as an individual or small-business person, quantum is likely to be something that proves immensely helpful only after industry-focused software interfaces have been created.

Industries Likely to Benefit

As the Chairman of The Futurist Institute, I directed an analysis and study of corporate and commercial opportunities in quantum computing across industries. The overview is in Figure 11-1. We identified a number of industries likely to benefit from the computational power promised by quantum computing. Most of these industries deal with large amounts of data.

The industries we have identified include the following: finance, government, transport and logistics (e.g., e-commerce), energy, healthcare, and agriculture. As you can see in Figure 11-1, finance is a field that is likely to be one of the most — if not the very most — affected by quantum computing.

Figure 11-1: Quantum Computing Assessment by Sector

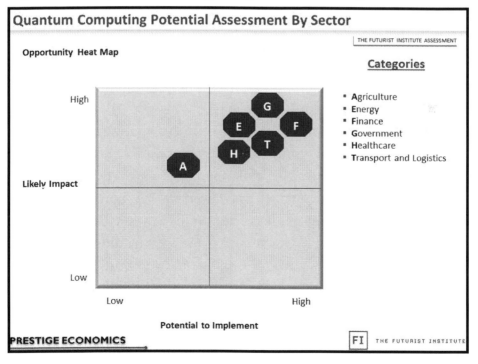

A number of the use cases are purely theoretical as a universal quantum computer with general-purpose applicability and integration with classical computing at a commercial scale does not yet exist.

Also, for the purposes of our analysis, we excluded hard science, engineering, and mathematic use cases even though these could benefit from quantum computing, with massive research and scientific implications. We excluded these from our analysis because they may take longer to impact professionals, businesses, and the economy at large.

For the main industries we considered, we paid close attention to the already-existing use cases for predictive data analytics, machine learning, and artificial intelligence solutions. We concluded that it seemed reasonable that quantum computing could take these efforts to the next level if and when quantum reaches full commercialization. And with quantum, real AI could become a much more attainable technology.

The Futurist Institute's Finance Quantum Assessment

As I noted previously, one of the professional fields with the highest number of use cases is finance, and we have identified 11 finance use cases for quantum computing in Figure 11-2. This should not be a surprise, because finance is often a field that is quick to embrace technology — especially for trading. The rise of algorithmic (or "algo") traders and technical trading has been well documented. Even my financial research firm, Prestige Economics, produces weekly technical analysis that taps into algo trading dynamics.

While data analysis, predictive data analytics, machine learning, and AI are not new, quantum computing could help financial market analysts reach more accurate forecasts more efficiently. This is a massively high-value use case for quantum computing.

After all, if you can have the most optimized — and fastest — trading model in the market, that usually contributes right to the bottom line of a trading firm. And the amount of data that can be looked at in financial markets is almost incomprehensible. Even the best models have some limitations as to the amount of data they may be able to incorporate. But with quantum computing, the volume of data that could be analyzed is likely to be much greater, which could help traders more accurately predict market price action. And reap bigger profits.

Figure 11-2: Finance Quantum Computing Potential

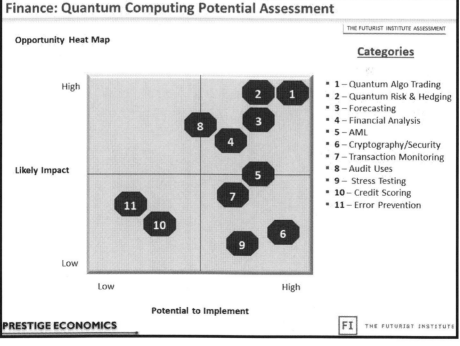

Although this use case may not be of the highest value for society as a whole, it is likely to be a high value use case for outright financial returns.

Similar to the use case for quantum algo trading — but with a higher societal benefit — would likely be quantum risk management and hedging strategies. This would likely involve using the same kind of market data as algo traders but with the purpose of reducing risks — especially for corporations. Firms face all kinds of risks, including interest rate, foreign exchange, and commodity price risks. When these firms miss these risks or get them wrong, it can adversely affect their profit margins. And people can lose their jobs. More effective and comprehensive risk management hedging strategies could help protect corporate profits and protect jobs.

Other related market-based use cases of quantum computing include forecasting and financial analysis. This could be related to forecasting or analyzing economic indicators, markets, companies, or indices. The exact use may not be as explicit as quantum algo or quantum hedging, but it is related.

In effect, these four use cases are designed to maximize returns in financial markets. They are also the four use cases with the highest potential to be implemented and the highest likely impacts.

The remaining seven use cases for quantum computing in finance are tied to protecting funds, regulatory needs, or otherwise securing the business of finance.

We see a high potential for implementation of (but a lower likely impact or financial return for) quantum in finance for AML (anti-money laundering), transaction monitoring, stress testing, and cryptography.

One use case with mixed potential for implementation, despite a potentially big impact, would be using quantum computing in audits. Accountants may lose their minds with excitement over the endless data that can be recorded on a blockchain, but using quantum in audits may be slower coming — even though it could be a valuable tool in sampling and testing audit processes.

The final two use cases for quantum computing in finance have a relatively lower implementation potential, and they also have potentially lower value as well. These are the use cases for quantum computing in error prevention and credit scoring.

The parallel non-deterministic processes of quantum computing that should help find errors and oddballs, as well as solutions to intractable problems with incomprehensible levels of data, make it an almost ideal fit for finance, from regulation and audit to trading and forecasting.

Threshold of Need

For most companies, near-term investing in quantum computing or installing quantum computers will not be a necessity — even if it were an option. The juice might just not be worth the squeeze, and it might be complete overkill. There is just not a high enough threshold of need.

Plus, for now, there is neither hardware nor software at a commercial level, let alone a very easy-to-use corporate interface or any quantum-reliant apps, that caters to the needs of any specific individuals or industries.

But they will likely come as quantum computing advances. And finance will be one of the fields at the forefront of quantum computing adoption in the decade ahead and beyond.

As with other topics in the future of finance, however, I must continue to underscore that it is important to place technological developments in a historical context. And quantum is likely to be a critical step change in technology.

But this time is never different.

Quantum computing offers the potential to be a step change in data processing and computational power. And yet quantum computing technology is also at risk from the hype locusts that consume promising technologies in a pump-and-dump investment cycle.

What comes next for quantum computing will be new. But it won't be the new internet or the new blockchain.

Quantum computing will, however, be a new way of computing that will be critical for fields with massive amounts of data, like finance. This is why quantum will become increasingly important for the future of finance — just as previous forms of computation have.

CHAPTER 12

CYBERSECURITY

Cybersecurity will be critical for the future of finance. Period.

It's part of the reason that I completed a certificate in cybersecurity at Carnegie Mellon University in 2018. At the end of the program, I had three big takeaways that are relevant for thinking about cybersecurity and the future of finance.

The first notion is the concept of **resilience**. This means, can your company bounce back? It is a question intrinsically linked at the hip with the notion of survivability. In other words, will your company survive a cyberattack, or will it cease to be a going concern? When I think of resilience, I think of a company that is able to respond quickly to a cyberattack so that it does not interrupt day-to-day operations — or result in lost customers.

The second concept that was put forward in the course was the notion of **resource management**. This is the idea that you cannot do everything you want with the security of a company. This will be one of the biggest challenges for finance companies in the decades to come.

After all, many executives repeatedly tell me that they could spend every dollar of their entire operating budget on cybersecurity and still not feel completely 100 percent comfortable with their risks and exposures. In the end, companies will be forced to make increasingly difficult choices about how to allocate resources for a non-revenue-generating activity like cybersecurity. And this will be doubly as critical in finance.

The third most important cybersecurity concept I took away from the course is **attack surface**, which is the amount of different points and places that an entity is exposed to a potential cyberattack. In any company, there are risks. And with a centralized network, it may be easier to control the flow of information and limit exposures.

Attack Surface and Blockchain Technology

With blockchain technology, the attack surface may actually be larger than with other databases. After all, the system is based on a distributed ledger among many parties. This means that using a system like blockchain to increase security of encryption and transparency of records may have the unintended adverse consequence of increasing a company's attack surface, potentially making it more vulnerable to cyberthreats.

If you work in a company where there's a finance department, it's pretty easy to track down someone in that department if there is a leak in of the shipping manifests and payment information. Yes, there is a central point of failure risk, but you have a small attack surface. You know who the few risks are.

But if you start sharing information across a broad, distributed network, there's a lot more risk. There would likely be more individuals with access to the blockchain who could share that sensitive information.

Rising Risks Tied to Quantum Computing
Quantum computing threatens to break blockchains, Bitcoin, and cryptocurrencies.

But it also threatens all other kinds of cryptography and encrypted data — everything from your email account to your bank accounts would be vulnerable. After all, decryption is one of the theoretically best and highest-value use cases for a quantum computer because of its ability to perform nondeterministic calculations in parallel.

One likely solution to quantum decryption threats could stem from the theory that there should be a future potential level of unconditional security provided by the use of quantum cryptography due to the same probabilistic nature of a quantum computing encryption system.[1]

In other words, while quantum computing threatens current cryptography and encryption, quantum computing could also be the future solution and replacement that counters those same threats.

La cryptographie est morte. Vive la cryptographie!

Quantum cryptography dates back to 1984, and the use of quantum key distribution could present a solution to the potential for quantum computing to crack modern cryptography.[2] But despite the tremendous value proposition of quantum encryption, it does not mean that everyone may need immediate access to quantum computers — or a combined regular processor and quantum processor known as a coprocessor. Some users will certainly come before others.

At the top of the upgrade-to-quantum-encryption cybersecurity list are computers that are critical for national security. This is particularly important because of the theoretical ability to use quantum computing to decrypt foreign communications — as well as protect our own communications.

Figure 12-1: Chinese Quantum Patents Outpace U.S. Patents[3]

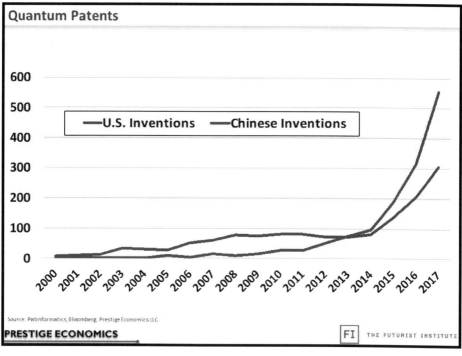

Winning the race to quantum computing is a critical prerequisite for the United States to maintain military supremacy. But the United States is at risk of losing the race to quantum computing, which can be seen in Figure 12-1. Chinese patents in the field of quantum have outpaced U.S. quantum patents significantly.

Quantum physics was one of four major scientific research programs highlighted in China's National Medium- and Long-Term Science and Technology Development Plan Outline (2006-2020). These concerns also appeared in the USTR report that preceded the Section 301 tariffs that the United States placed on China in 2018.[4] Plus, the U.S. Trade Czar, Peter Navarro, has frequently highlighted the risks of losing the technology race with China — including the race to quantum computing. Navarro has voiced these types of concerns in his books, among other places.[5]

In short, China could win the race to quantum.

Resilience and Finance

Although national security may be at the top of the list of industries seeking to acquire quantum computing technology, finance is likely to be not too far behind.

After all, if we again consider the concept of *resilience*, it should be clear that companies that suffer massive security breeches could cease to be going concerns. For finance, being able to protect retail and institutional client data and financial accounts is a core fiduciary duty. And banks will be high-value targets in a quantum decryption world.

When I think of resilience, I think of the hope that quantum encryption could make information safer. And financial institutions will see this as an absolutely critical priority.

The push to quantum computers will also likely be particularly high in the United States. As you can see in Figure 12-2, the United States already faces the highest per capita cybersecurity costs in the world — and that's without quantum computers. Plus, as you can see in Figure 12-3, China is the source of almost twice as many cyberattacks as the United States.

These two factors make the U.S. government concerned about a future in which China might win the race to quantum. But it should also make U.S. financial institutions very nervous.

Figure 12-2: Per Capita Cost of Cyberattacks[6]

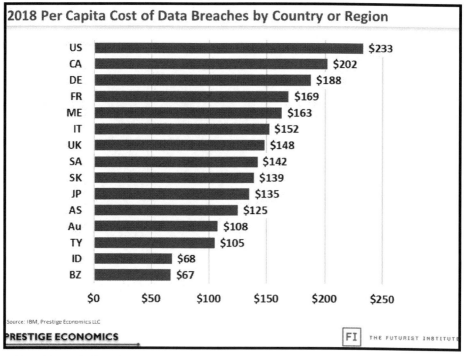

Resource Management and Cybersecurity Strategy

Of course, financial institutions will still need to consider the implications of *resource management*. This is the idea that you cannot do everything you want with the security of a company.

And the same, of course, is true when considering the use of quantum computing for commercial and corporate purposes in terms of time, processing power, and cost. Sometimes the juice is not worth the squeeze — and quantum is not for everything. But it is likely to be critical for finance.

The same is true, of course, with government budgets as well. The amount of resources dedicated to cybersecurity has been increasing, both for governments and as a percent of U.S. GDP.

Figure 12-3: Cyberattack Origins[7]

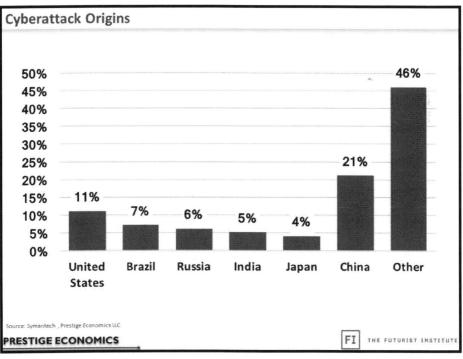

In Figure 12-4, you can see the planned acceleration of U.S. government spending on cybersecurity. And in Figure 12-5, you can see how cybersecurity spending as a percent of U.S. GDP has also been rising. And beyond the national security implications for cybersecurity, it's important to realize that the United States is already dedicating a lot of resources to fending off cyberattacks. And while the United States is concerned about China getting quantum computing first, the European Union is concerned about "potential American dominance" in quantum computing.[8]

It's difficult to really say that quantum computing will trigger a global cybersecurity arms race because cybersecurity is already is a global cybersecurity arms race in play.

Figure 12-4: U.S. Government Spending on Cybersecurity[9]

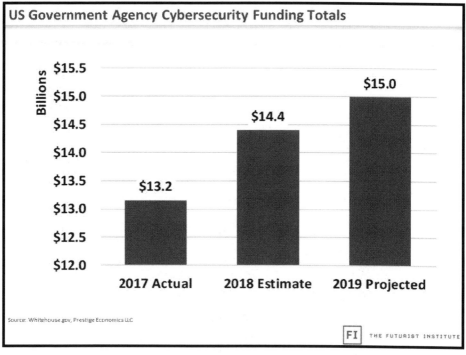

This is why governments as well as companies — especially financial institutions — are spending massive sums and dedicating significant resources on cybersecurity.

Attack Surface

In economic terms, the entire economy is the attack surface when it comes to cyberthreats, and financial institutions are particularly attractive targets. But the current attack surface is protected by encryptions and cybersecurity that are currently effective against most conventional cyberattacks.

But once quantum cyberattacks become a possibility, much of the attack surface could be vulnerable. And the ability to do material damage with quantum cyberattacks will increase exponentially.

Figure 12-5: Cybersecurity Spending as a Percent of GDP[10]

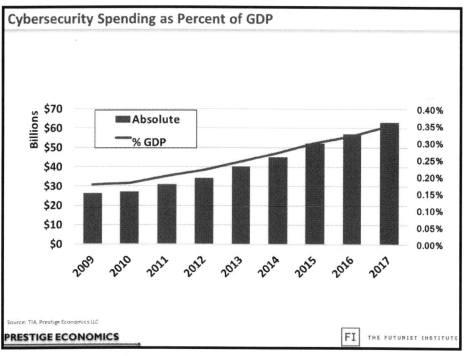

Failure is Not an Option

Corporations — and especially financial institutions — will need to swiftly adopt quantum encryptions to protect themselves from quantum cyberattacks. But these companies must begin preparing now for a switch to quantum encryption now — before the step change to quantum cryptography even happens. And if they are caught behind, the impact could be catastrophic.

One science writer for *The New York Times* noted that the difference between quantum computing and classical computing is like the difference between nuclear power and fire. When considering quantum computing as nuclear strength, the stakes become a bit clearer: They couldn't be higher.

Considering the Upside

In early 2019, I gave a speech in New York City to a group of Chief Information Officers (CIOs) from various financial institutions. And I shared with them a number of topics I have discussed in this book. To my surprise, they seemed quite distraught by the information I shared, so I tried to lighten the mood by pointing out how critical CIOs and Chief Information Security Officers — CISOs — will be in the future of finance.

That notion got quite a few laughs. Because it was true.

Someday, finance companies may have very few traders, analysts, and asset managers. But as finance becomes increasingly digital, the importance of CIOs and CISOs will grow. In fact, they are likely to be the professionals with the greatest level of future job security in the entire world of finance.

CHAPTER 13

ROBO-ADVISORS

Robo-advising is the catch-all term for automated trading programs that retail investors use to make investments. These robos manage trades, and they are often based on technical, algo, or black box models. Essentially, math and equations underpin their trading.

They are another form of passive asset management. But they are also exposed to retail investors. And this might be a problem.

A couple of years ago, one of my colleagues and I called several robo-advisors and we got sales representatives on the phone who were encouraging us to use their platforms. Almost everyone we spoke to had no idea how their particular robo-advisor worked.

If we asked about strategy, the people on the phone did not know the difference between a long fund and a long-short fund. Furthermore, some people we spoke to conflated the notion of a goal fund (what people in financial services usually call a target fund) and a gold fund.

Even in late 2017, I had a conversation with someone from FINRA who told me that despite the almost persistent rise in U.S. equities during that year, the number of complaints and lawsuits against robo-advisors was rising.

This begs the question: What will happen in a downturn?

In my opinion, people lost trust in financial institutions during the Great Recession of 2007-2009. And they turned to technology rather than people. But they have clearly placed too much faith in technology. And the people who interface with customers, in my own personal experience, may lack the knowledge to effectively fulfill the fiduciary duty of a financial planner or advisor.

This means that the future of finance for robo-advising is likely to have a moment of tears. Whenever the next downturn comes, there are likely to be many individual losses by retail investors. And some class action lawsuits are likely to follow.

But in the longer run, I think digital market access will proliferate and expand in a way that gives individuals a lot more control — and liability — for their own decisions. But that would defeat the purpose of blindly trusting technology over skilled professionals performing a fiduciary duty. And that is where robo-advising generally appears to be right now.

The next major downturn is likely to show something that institutional investors have long known: Not all funds or advisors are equal. Those that come out on top in a downturn could come to dominate the now still-fragmented robo-advisor marketplace.

CHAPTER 14

BIASED AI

There is a not-small group of market observers out in the world who expect something called the Robocalypse.

These would-be prophets dismally predict that computers will run amok, destroying the world and all the people in it. This is the well from which every Robocalypse film springs (e.g., *The Terminator*). And while there is some reason to be concerned, Robocalypse claims are extreme.

Unfortunately, we need look no further than the miserable failure of Microsoft's attempt to expose its artificial intelligence (AI) pet project, Tay, to the world via Twitter. In less than a day, Tay had learned some very bad things like racism, rabid anti-Semitism, and other forms of unfiltered hate.[1]

Naturally, the project was shut down quickly. At the time, which was several years ago now, I noted that I expected it would be some time before anyone lets its AI project out in public again. We haven't seen another such project since.

The risk that computers will run amok is a problem that highlights the increasingly important need for project management — and oversight for anything that looks even remotely like an independently functioning computer program.

While the prospects of a computer program becoming murderous toward humanity or taking on the mantle of a digital Nazi are less of a concern in the field of finance, the need to monitor technical and algo trading platforms is — and will be — critical for the future of finance.

Furthermore, from a legal standpoint, the use of AI in financial institutions is likely to occur within highly regulated environments to ensure that historical biases, which may have been ingrained in past systems and data by individuals operating with now illegal biases, are not perpetuated further in the present and future.

Imagine a lending institution using an AI program that was making individual mortgage and lending calculations based on historical data that was informed by redlining and institutional racism.

Essentially, that financial institution would be perpetuating those policies by using data from that era. In a way, dirty data could very well have tainted the models that informed the machine learning and predictive analytics that became foundational for the AI created by that financial institution.

Furthermore, that institution could find itself on the other end of a civil rights lawsuit. Even though no individual person may have intentionally made a judgement that supported redlining or any other racist policies, the computer program may have used such data and reinforced such policies in its decision making.

Make no mistake, lawsuits around AI decisions will happen in coming years and decades.

And they will become a risk to institutions in the future of finance.

I also expect these kinds of lawsuits could occur in financial institutions as well as many other organizations where AI programs are used. And these kinds of suits could impact a wide swath of operational and administrative areas, from lending decisions and business practices to vendor selection and human resources.

As of the writing of this book, the European Union had already taken big steps to prevent issues with AI programs that could effectively limit their use in future lending and finance decisions.

As you can see, even though the future of finance will include more automation, it could also include additional legal risks. This means that financial institutions will have to do internal cost-benefit analyses to see if AI programs will actually save them money and have a big enough value impact to justify a greater risk of legal exposure.

CHAPTER 15

DEBT AND ENTITLEMENTS

One of the biggest challenges for the future of finance is the rising U.S. national debt. Every economist, FOMC member, and Fed Chair warns about the negative impact high levels of debt are likely to have on long-term growth rates. But these warnings go largely unheeded, leaving dismal scientists to play Cassandra.[1]

The U.S. national debt is a growing problem. At almost $22.5 trillion, the national debt is not a small sum. In fact, it comes out to over $68,300 for every man, woman, and child living in the United States of America.[2]

That is a lot of debt!

As you can see in Figure 15-1, the pace at which the U.S. national debt is rising has accelerated. It took 205 years for the U.S. national debt to exceed $1 trillion, which happened in October 1981. But it then took less than five years for the national debt to double to $2 trillion in April 1986. The most recent doubling of the U.S. national debt occurred during the current business cycle — in the wake of the Great Recession.[3]

Although not as pronounced as the trend in total U.S. government debt, the debt-to-GDP ratio has also risen sharply since the onset of the Great Recession in December 2007 (Figure 15-2).

One major negative impact of a high national debt is the drag on potential future U.S. economic growth as measured by Gross Domestic Product — or GDP. Plus, debt exposures can be exacerbated by compounding interest on already outstanding government debt.

Although some analysts are quick to note that the U.S. debt-to-GDP ratio is lower than other countries, it is also important to note that the U.S. economy is the largest in the world. This means that rising U.S. debt levels could make it more difficult for the global economy to absorb U.S. debt issuances over time.

2017 Tax Reform in Context
U.S. tax reform legislation that was passed in 2017 was lauded as a once-in-a-generation tax cut, which it was. While the reforms changed taxation laws, limits, and brackets for many different kinds of taxes, the legislation did not address entitlements. And payroll taxes were never discussed. Yet some of the biggest risks to the national debt and long-term potential GDP growth of the U.S. economy will hinge on addressing underfunded entitlements expenditures and fighting to contain the U.S. national debt.

To cover ballooning entitlements expenditures, payroll taxes could rise sharply, which could exacerbate the tax burden on workers, the self-employed, and people in the gig economy. This would not be a great look for the future of the U.S. economy.

Figure 15-1: Total U.S. Federal Debt[4]

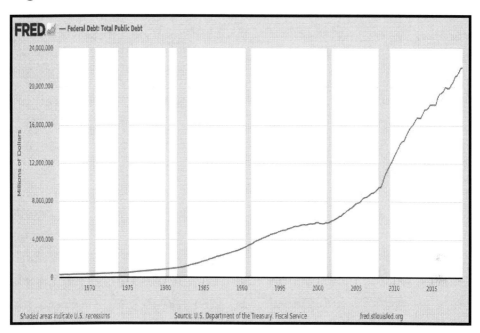

Figure 15-2: Total U.S. Federal Debt as a Percent of GDP[5]

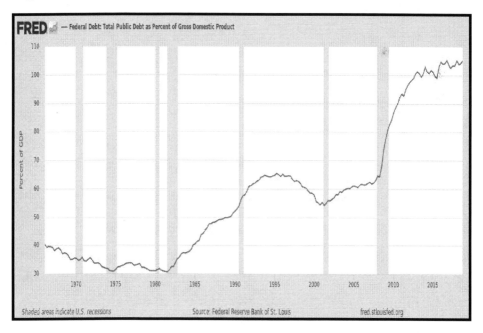

Without a reform of the entitlement system, increasingly high levels of government debt and changing demographics are likely to drive up interest rates and payroll taxes. Furthermore, a greater level of debt and higher payroll taxes could contribute to an acceleration of automation — and a reduction of jobs for people over time. Without a proactive approach, this could become unsustainable for the U.S. labor market, economy, and society.

These issues were not addressed by the self-proclaimed fiscally conservative Republican Party when it had control of both chambers of the legislature and the office of the presidency. This leaves me very concerned about prospects for these issues over the next decade. And it makes one thing seem certain: The 2020 presidential election is also unlikely to change these issues.

Risks of Debt
The problem with a rising U.S. national debt is that it can drive up interest rates. After all, as the supply of government bonds rises, the price will fall (as in all markets). And for bonds, when prices fall, interest rates rise. This means that, over time, the net interest payments on U.S. debt are likely to rise. Allocating an increasing percentage of GDP to interest payments would clearly be bad for long-term potential U.S. GDP growth.

The risk of recession would further increase the likelihood that the debt level and the debt-to-GDP ratio would rise between 2020 and 2024. Even without a recession, the level of the national debt and the national debt as a percent of GDP are likely to rise significantly during the current presidential tenure.

And entitlements are a major source of additional imminent debt. Unfortunately, while the U.S. national debt is large, the unfunded financial obligations stemming from U.S. entitlements are much larger — and are likely to compound U.S. debt problems in coming years. Simply put, entitlements pose the greatest threat to future U.S. government debt levels — and U.S. economic growth.

Entitlements

U.S. entitlements, including Medicare, Medicaid, and Social Security, are financed by payroll taxes from workers. Payroll taxes are separate from income taxes, and while income tax rates have fallen on fiscal policy changes, payroll taxes are on a one-way trip higher. You see, entitlements are wildly underfunded.

All the sovereign debt in the world totals around $60 trillion.[6] That is the debt cumulatively held by all national governments in the world. But the size of unfunded U.S. entitlements might be more than three times that level. That's right: the unfunded, off-balance sheet obligations for Medicare, Medicaid, and Social Security could be $200 trillion.[7]

This level of off-balance sheet debt obligation existentially threatens the U.S. economy. The Heritage Foundation has taken calculations from the U.S. Congressional Budget Office about entitlements to create Figure 15-3, which looks quite catastrophic. Basically, by 2030, all U.S. tax revenue will be consumed by entitlements and the interest on the national debt. And these were the dismal calculations before tax reform and recent U.S. budgets started increasing the national debt even more rapidly.

The year 2030 is not that far in the future, and the clock is ticking.

But despite the magnitude of the entitlements problem, do not expect this to be an issue that will be seriously addressed during or following the 2020 presidential election.

The Grandfather of U.S. Social Security

Part of the problem with entitlements stems from their origins. The U.S. Social Security Administration website credits Otto von Bismarck as the grandfather of U.S. entitlements.[8]

Bismarck's portrait is even on the U.S. Social Security Administration's website (Figure 15-4).

Figure 15-3: Tax Revenue Spent on Entitlements[9]

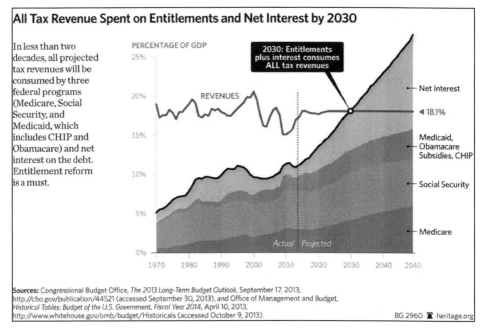

Bismarck was a powerful politician known for his use of *Realpolitik*, a political doctrine built on pragmatism to advance national self-interests. For him, entitlements were convenient and expedient. Unfortunately, that is no longer the case. Today, entitlements threaten to crush the U.S. economy with increased levels of debt.

And without reform, they could decimate the U.S. workforce.

Bismarck's system was also sustainable. His system guaranteed a pension to German workers over 70, but the average life expectancy in Germany in the late 1880s was only 40.[10] In other words, so few people were expected to receive the benefits that the program's cost would be negligible.

Figure 15-4: Grandfather of Social Security, Otto von Bismarck[11]

Bismarck rigged entitlements to help crush his political opponents without having to pay out. But the current entitlement system in the United States is an unfunded off-balance sheet liability that threatens to crush the entire economy and usher in a labor market Robocalypse. Plus, fixing entitlements presents a horrible dilemma as many Americans rely heavily on entitlements for income (Figure 15-5).

But how did this system break down? Bismarck had such a good thing going. What happened?

This can be answered in one word: demographics.

Figure 15-5: Expected Importance of Social Security[12]

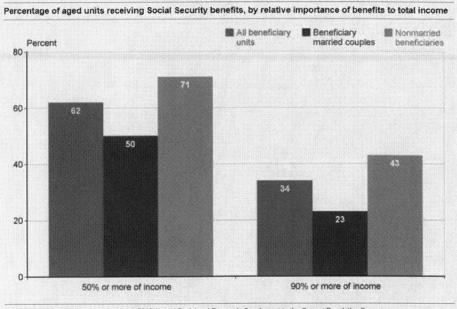

Demographics

U.S. population growth has slowed sharply, and this demographic shift appears unstoppable. Plus, as birthrates have fallen, life expectancy has also risen. This compounds the funding shortfalls for entitlements. Worse still: No president, senator, or congressman can change U.S. demographics. This is bigger than one person.

And its discussion is unlikely to be anywhere near the 2020 presidential election — and other coming elections as well.

Population growth in the United States has fallen from annual rates of over 1.5 percent per year during the 1950s and early 1960s to just 0.7 percent since 2011.[13] Some of this slowing in population growth is due to a decline in the U.S. fertility rate. In general, fertility rates have been dropping globally, but according to demographer Jonathan Last, the U.S. fertility rate is still relatively high at 1.93.[14]

However, even though the U.S. total fertility rate is relatively high compared to other industrialized nations, it is below the 2.1 percent "golden number" required to maintain a population, according to Last.[15]

This is a huge problem for maintaining entitlements. After all, the entitlement system worked really well in 1940, when there were 159.4 workers per beneficiary (Figure 15-6). But it is more challenging since that number fell to only 2.8 in 2013. Plus, it is likely to fall to 2 workers per beneficiary by 2040.[16]

Entitlements are under siege from both sides: The birthrate has fallen and life expectancy has risen

In addition to lower birthrates, U.S. life expectancy has doubled since Bismarck implemented entitlements in Germany in 1889 — from around 40 years to above 80 years. Plus, the age at which people receive U.S. entitlements benefits has actually been lowered from 70 to 65. On top of a significantly larger population being eligible to receive entitlements, the medical costs required to support an aging population have also risen.

Figure 15-6: Ratio of Workers to Social Security Beneficiaries[17]

Year	Covered Workers (in thousands)	Beneficiaries (in thousands)	Ratio
1940	35,390	222	159.4
1945	46,390	1,106	41.9
1950	48,280	2,930	16.5
1955	65,200	7,563	8.6
1960	72,530	14,262	5.1
1965	80,680	20,157	4.0
1970	93,090	25,186	3.7
1975	100,200	31,123	3.2
1980	113,656	35,118	3.2
1985	120,565	36,650	3.3
1990	133,672	39,470	3.4
1995	141,446	43,107	3.3
2000	155,295	45,166	3.4
2005	159,081	48,133	3.3
2010	156,725	53,398	2.9
2013	163,221	57,471	2.8

Everything might be OK — if U.S. population growth were extremely robust. But it is not. Plus, the current administration is pushing hard to reduce illegal immigration to the United States. While this can have some benefits for society and the economy in some ways, it can also reduce the pace of population growth and lower the average U.S. birthrate.

Population growth has slowed to less than half the rate seen during the baby boom years, and the total U.S. fertility rate is below the "golden number" that is required to maintain a population. As Last notes, "Social Security is, in essence, a Ponzi scheme. Like all Ponzi schemes, it works just fine — so long as the intake of new participants continues to increase."[18] Unfortunately, entitlements are nearing a breaking point.

A big problem with slowing birthrates is the manifestation of a shrinking tax base at the same time that unfunded financial obligations are rising. This means that the unfunded $200 trillion or more in future entitlements payments will be borne by an increasingly smaller proportion of workers in the population. And as the population ages, there is another issue: Who will do the work? The answer is simple: We will create jobs for robots.

Payroll Taxes and a Shrinking U.S. Tax Base
When there is a tax shortfall, there is often a need to raise taxes. And there are risks of significantly higher payroll taxes in the not-too-distant future. Slowing population growth is likely to exacerbate U.S. debt and entitlement burdens by accelerating the reduction in the U.S. tax base — especially for payroll taxes, which fund entitlements. This could justify raising payroll taxes.

So, who pays payroll taxes?

Employees split entitlement costs with their employers, who pay half. This means that if entitlement costs rise, the cost for an employer to keep a person employed will also increase. The substitution effect of automation for labor would then likely accelerate because of the financial incentives in place for employers.

As payroll taxes increase to cover the costs associated with underfunded entitlements, the financial incentives for employers to shift work away from human laborers and add technology are likely to be reinforced. A number of my clients have shared their concerns about the risk of rising costs associated with health care costs for their workers.

How do you think employers will feel about the burden of paying much higher payroll taxes? They do pay half of them, after all.

Automation

As U.S. population growth slows and older workers age out of the workforce, automation could provide a solution. Automation has the potential to contribute significantly to U.S. economic growth.

But while automation solves some of the demographic problems we have in the United States, it threatens to exacerbate some of the entitlement problems. And unreformed entitlements present a significant risk of over-automation to the U.S. economy. If you were to think of the most important benefits you get as an employee, you might think of time off or sick days.

But your employer probably thinks about the most expensive items first: payroll taxes and health care. Kiosks and robots don't get time off, they certainly don't require health care costs, and they aren't subject to payroll taxes — for now.

In mid-2016, unemployment in Spain was around 20 percent,[19] and youth unemployment was around 43 percent.[20] So there were a lot of people available to work. But in Barcelona, Spain, during the summer of 2016, kiosks were in use at the airport's Burger King restaurant.

In Spain, as in much of Europe, the cost to hire someone can be prohibitive compared to the United States. And kiosks require no payroll taxes, no health insurance costs, no government entitlements, no vacation, and no sick days. With kiosks replacing workers, youth unemployment is unlikely to get significantly better. This also bodes ill for U.S. youth participation and unemployment rates. Be advised: Fast food robots (among others) are coming.

Entrepreneurs at Risk

Rising entitlement costs and payroll taxes could also stifle entrepreneurship. Unlike employees, who split payroll tax obligations with their employers, self-employed people bear the full brunt of payroll taxes personally. The rate is currently 15.3 percent of income.[21] In the future, that rate will rise faster for entrepreneurs since they will not be splitting the increase in payroll taxes with an employer. If entitlements are not drastically overhauled, a self-employment tax rate of 25 percent by 2030 is not inconceivable.

Increasingly high self-employment tax rates are likely to stifle entrepreneurship and hurt self-employed workers. According to an article by the Pew Foundation, the percent of workers who are self-employed fell from 11.4 percent in 1990 to 10 percent in 2014.[22] More importantly, the Pew Foundation notes that 30 percent of U.S. jobs are held "by the self-employed and the workers they hire."[23] In other words, in 2014, 14.6 million self-employed workers hired another 29.4 million workers, accounting for 30 percent of the entire U.S. workforce.

With the prospect of entitlement shortfalls and a shrinking tax base, self-employment tax rates are going to rise.

The impact of these additional costs is likely to engender a continued downward trend in the percent of self-employed workers. Plus, workers in the so-called gig economy — like all 1099s — are also subject to self-employment taxes. This could also make the existence of the gig economy less tenable in the future as payroll taxes rise.

The labor force participation rate is also at risk as the population ages further, unfunded entitlements rise, and the potential for overincentivized automation increases.

The labor force participation rate is a measure of what percentage of the able-bodied civilian population is working or looking for work. I also expect youth participation rates will continue to fall as younger workers are crowded out by older workers and automation.

Other Unfunded Obligations

As tax incentives present risks that workers could be crowded out by automation, consider also that the $200 trillion figure for unfunded entitlements does not take into account pension data for federal, state, county, or city government employees. Many of these workers also have defined benefits pensions that are underfunded — and in great need of reform. The gap in funds for these pensions will also likely incentivize automation and drive jobs for robots — rather than jobs for people.

There is an old joke that the best kind of autoworker to be is a retired autoworker. Without a reform of entitlements and defined benefits plans, the joke could be rewritten as the best kind of any U.S. worker to be will be a retired U.S. worker. This will affect all of us since unfunded off-balance sheet obligations could necessitate that government and private pension benefits be drastically reduced (especially for future generations) while contribution costs rise further. Problems beget problems.

Summary

Rising debt levels in the United States present long-term risks to growth. The surprise with the 2017 tax cuts was that despite Republican stewardship of the initiative, they were unbalanced.

As an economist, I see tax cuts as good. But I also see more debt as bad. Unfortunately, the tax reform of 2017 included both tax cuts — and more debt.

Plus, the most recent budgets during the current term of the Trump administration also included significant increases in the national debt. This means that even if Trump is reelected, there may still be a need to "pork up" future budgets.

In the longer term, declines in birthrates, increased longevity, rising health care costs, falling labor force participation rates, and overincentivized automation are likely to accelerate and exacerbate the problems of the U.S. national defined benefits programs known as entitlements — programs that worked best financially when the age at which one received benefits exceeded life expectancy by 30 years.

But the entitlements system was ignored during the 2016 presidential election, during the 2017 tax reform, and in the 2018 midterms. It is likely to remain ignored for as long as possible — and likely through the 2020 presidential election cycle.

The Future Impacts of Entitlements
Just because politicians want to play the game of see no evil, hear no evil, speak no evil does not mean that in fact there is no evil.

In truth, massive unfunded off-balance sheet debt obligations — à la entitlements — could eventually subvert stable Western financial systems, eradicating economic growth and introducing destabilizing factors that could subvert democracy itself.

Some reading this may see my views here as hyperbole. And believe me, I wish they were. But sadly, they are not.

In order to finance shortfalls no one wants to address, the eventual impact could be very painful — and it could come sooner than many expect — like in-the-next-decade-or-so sooner.

This means by 2030, payroll taxes may find themselves closer to 25 percent than 15 percent. And that could have a deleterious effect on American workers, U.S.-based corporations, and U.S. equity markets.

On a global scale, these problems are even worse in some European countries, which means that the problems we have been ignoring could drastically impact economic and business growth expectations globally — especially in consumer-driven service economies, where drastically reduced incomes of retirees could dovetail with significantly increased payroll taxes for prime-age workers.

For the future of the economy and financial markets, the impact of these risks cannot be understated.

CHAPTER 16

CENTRAL BANK BALANCE SHEETS

One of the biggest challenges in the wake of the financial crisis was how to stimulate economic growth at a time of almost unprecedented slowing. Expanding central bank balance sheets was one of the unprecedented critical solutions that the U.S. Federal Reserve, the Bank of England, the European Central Bank, the Bank of Japan, and other central banks took to keep their economies afloat.

And as we think about the future of finance, it is important to know that the trend of ever-expanding central bank balance sheets has already started — and it is likely to continue in the future.

The fact that central banks have been able to conjure funds from the ether in order to buy various assets from mortgage-backed securities (MBS) and Treasuries to corporate debt and equities is disconcerting. But it was highly effective, and it is therefore likely to occur again in the future. After all, if it works, why stop now?

This reality supports some of the economic arguments in favor of cryptocurrencies.

In fact, the first Bitcoin transaction, which is often referred to as the Genesis Block, included the following message:

The Times 03/Jan/2009 Chancellor on brink of second bailout for banks[1]

The Bank of England engaged in multiple bailouts and a 300 percent expansion in the size of its balance sheet between 2007 and 2012, from around 94 billion British pounds to over 400 billion, as you can see in Figure 16-1.

Figure 16-1: Bank of England Balance Sheet[2]

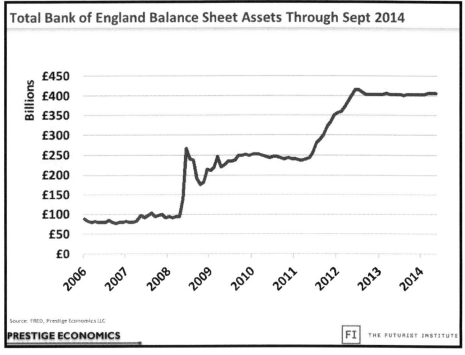

But the Bank of England was not alone in taking these kinds of measures. The European Central Bank also increased its balance sheet massively. The ECB expanded its balance sheet from 1.3 trillion euros in January 2008 to 3.1 trillion euros in June 2012. Then, from June 2012 until September 2014, the ECB reduced its balance sheet by about one-third — letting it fall from 3.1 trillion euros to 2.0 trillion euros.

During that time, however, the Eurozone economy slowed, and the Eurozone manufacturing PMI also conveyed a significant slowdown. The risk of a triple-dip recession in the Eurozone increased. As a result of this sharp slowdown, the ECB switched gears and rapidly expanded its balance sheet, which rose to almost 4.7 trillion euros by June 2019.

Figure 16-2: European Central Bank Balance Sheet[3]

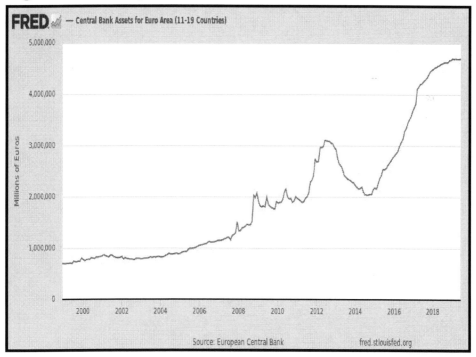

The expansion of central bank balance sheets was enacted as an extreme means to lower interest rates and indirectly stimulate financial activity and economic growth. This was achieved by having a central bank engage in buying government debt, mortgages, bonds, or equities. Each major central bank took a slightly different approach.

The most aggressive central bank expansion was implemented by the Bank of Japan, the quantitative easing program of which has included significant purchases of Japanese real estate investment trusts, known as J-REITs, as well as exchange-traded funds, or ETFs, of Japanese equities. In other words, the Bank of Japan has been a big buyer of Japanese equities.

Figure 16-3: Bank of Japan Balance Sheet[4]

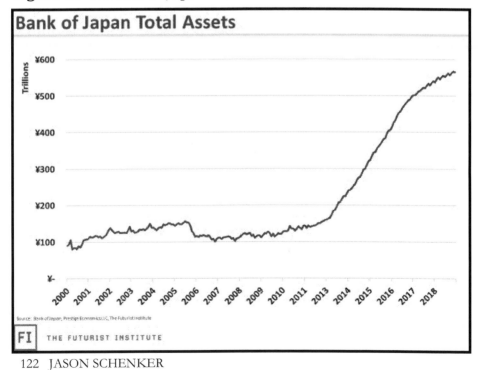

In 2010, the BoJ did not own any ETFs, but by March 2011, the BoJ's ownership of ETFs had increased to 185 billion Japanese yen. By September 2016, it had risen to over 11 trillion JPY. In September 2018, the BoJ owned almost 29 trillion JPY worth of ETFs. And the BoJ is now a major shareholder of many equities.

This situation is unprecedented and precarious, and it forces us to ask some difficult questions: How will the Bank of Japan extricate itself from Japanese equity markets? Will the BoJ ever be able to sell its equities? Will other central banks get themselves into a similar pickle? It is difficult to predict what will happen to Japanese equity markets if the BoJ steps back. But it does seem likely that other central banks could someday go down this path and buy equities as well.

Figure 16-4: BoJ Balance Sheet ETF Holdings[5]

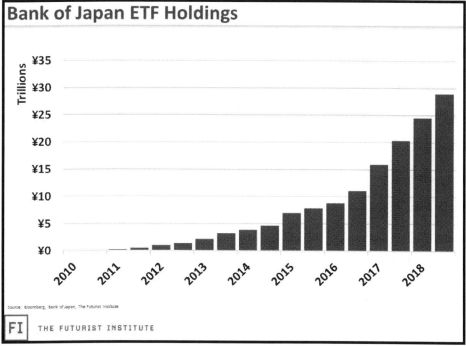

Source: Bloomberg, Bank of Japan, The Futurist Institute

FI THE FUTURIST INSTITUTE

The Federal Reserve

In response to slow growth after the Great Recession, the U.S. Federal Reserve engaged in purchasing mortgage-backed securities as a means to push down mortgage rates and stimulate housing activity in the United States. The Fed also purchased Treasuries, which pushed down interest rates — even after the federal funds rate was set by the Federal Reserve at zero percent.

The Fed increased its balance sheet in 2008 from around $900 billion in January 2008 to around a peak of $4.5 trillion by January 2015. But the Fed did not buy equities or corporate bonds, although that is something that it may consider doing in the future. Presently, however, the Fed is focused on reducing the level of its balance sheet, which now still sits above $3.8 trillion. But in the future, it is likely to expand its balance sheet again.

Figure 16-5: Total Fed Balance Sheet Assets[6]

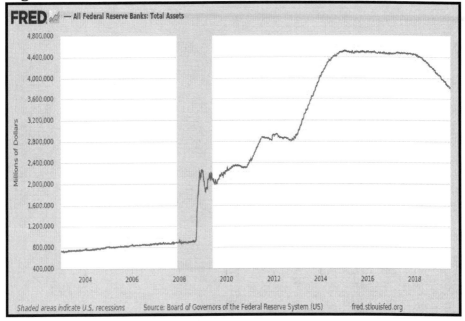

Beginning in October 2017, the U.S. Fed began reducing its balance sheet in a formal policy of balance sheet reductions by reducing reinvestment of maturing mortgage-backed securities and Treasuries. However, unlike the European Central Bank's attempt to reduce its balance sheet between 2012 and 2014, the Fed deliberately planned a very slow pace of balance sheet reductions. It was, I believe, in part due to the disastrous experience of the ECB that the Fed decided to be especially cautious in reducing the size of its own balance sheet.

The Future of Quantitative Easing

Even though the Fed has been reducing its balance sheet, the balance sheet is likely to remain at or near historically high levels for a long time to come. And it is likely to expand further in the future — rather than see declines down to levels seen before the Great Recession, which lasted from December 2007 to June 2009.

Expanding the Fed's balance sheet was highly effective at stimulating the U.S. economy. In other words, quantitative easing works. This means that the Fed is likely to expand its balance sheet again in the future.

Furthermore, Janet Yellen noted at the annual Kansas City Fed event in Jackson Hole, Wyoming in 2016 that "I expect that forward guidance and asset purchases will remain important components of the Fed's policy toolkit."

She further added that "Future policymakers may wish to explore the possibility of purchasing a broader range of assets."[7]

In other words, the Fed is not just likely to engage in quantitative easing again in the future, but the Fed is likely to buy different kinds of securities in the future as well. Even though Fed policy got tighter in 2017 and 2018, it is likely to be much looser again in the future.

Central Bank Balance Sheets and Cryptocurrencies

The expansion of central bank balance sheets is fundamentally supportive of the economic and financial arguments in favor of Bitcoin and digital currencies that are not backed by central banks. The impact of the expansions and persistently high levels of central bank balance sheets of the ECB and the Bank of England is unclear.

What is clear, however, is that central banks have cracked open the QE cookie jar — and that they are likely to spend more money they don't have, effectively creating the ability to purchase assets out of thin air.

There is no problem, however, from an accounting standpoint, if the assets eventually expire in value and fall off the balance sheet. But that is not going to be the case with the balance sheet of the Bank of Japan, which includes significant equity assets.

As we look ahead to the future of finance and the future of quantitative easing, one of the things I often speak about is a risk that with each cyclical downturn in the future, central banks may continue to expand their balance sheets.

As long as they are all doing this, however, it may not drastically impact foreign exchange rates. After all, if everyone plays the game, it's tougher for there to be an outright winner — or loser.

And they will all want to play the quantitative easing game again if they can.

The Future Quantum State of the U.S. Economy

The dynamics I have just described could eventually result in something I refer to as the future quantum state of the economy. As the U.S. Federal Reserve buys more assets during each downturn with money that it pulled out of nowhere, the central bank's balance sheet will grow and grow.

And if former Fed Chair Yellen's comments are to be believed, the Fed will eventually need to diversify the kinds of assets it buys, which could include everything from corporate debt to equities, as other central banks have done. But with each cycle, the central bank will become increasingly important as the buyer of last resort so that the U.S. economy becomes too big to fail.

This could also become extremely challenging, as the U.S. national debt rises due to unfunded entitlements and interest.

One potential worst-case scenario is where the central bank — after decades of cycles — eventually owns almost everything in the economy. And it will have paid for the debt, MBS, Treasuries, equities, and maybe even physical assets on its balance sheet with money it created — with money it didn't have in the first place.

This is effectively how we could have a quantum state of the economy, where the central bank owns everything with nothing.

Then we would have a big problem.

How central banks restore confidence in the fact that they won't go down this path will be a critical priority in the decade ahead.

And if they fail, this doomsday scenario could very well come to pass.

CHAPTER 17

UNIVERSAL BASIC INCOME

Universal basic income (UBI) is the notion that everyone will be paid a flat salary, regardless of whether or not they work. And the biggest problem with universal basic income is that we simply cannot afford it. As you saw in the Chapter 15, U.S. entitlement obligations, which could be as high as $200 trillion, make a further expansion of U.S. budgetary obligations for UBI virtually impossible.

According to David Freedman, who wrote an article on the subject for *MIT Technology Review*, an annual payment of $10,000 to every adult American "would be at least twice as expensive as current antipoverty benefits and overhead, adding between one and two trillion dollars to the federal budget."[1] Furthermore, Freedman argues that "existing safety-net programs could be expanded and tuned to eliminate poverty about as effectively but much less expensively, and they could continue to focus on providing jobs and the incentives to take them."[2] In other words, the inefficient programs in place could be better than UBI. Yikes!

Risks Beyond Cost

Aside from the cost of UBI, which is insurmountable, there are four major problems with UBI:

Inflation would rise.

Taxes would rise.

Long-term economic development could be stifled.

Society could become fractured.

European Attitudes

In Figure 17-1, you can see the results of a survey from a few years ago in which Europeans voiced support for universal basic income. However, despite this support, UBI has so far failed when voters went to the ballot box to vote on the idea. As such, not one single nation has voted to approve this policy.

The entire concept of UBI smacks of full-blown communism, with a redistribution of income. Perhaps this is why Europeans, who have a more colorful political history than Americans, find it to be an appealing option. However, it is more likely that UBI finds support in Europe because the same respondents who support UBI do not actually fully understand it. This is shown in Figure 17-2.

I wager that graphs of European opinions and knowledge about communism during the 1920s may have looked somewhat similar. For my European friends, as well as my American ones, let us now consider some costs of UBI that go beyond the budget.

Figure 17-1: Europeans Who Would Vote for Basic Income[3]

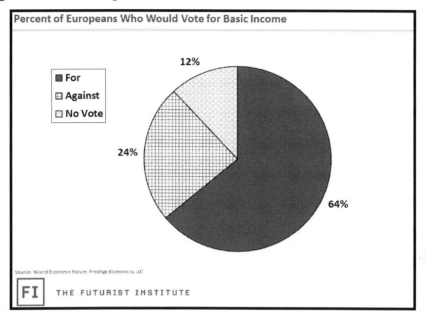

Figure 17-2: Europeans Familiar With Basic Income[4]

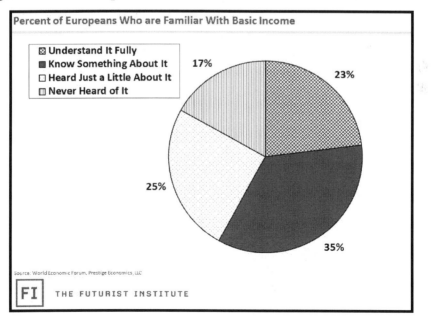

Inflation

Inflation is when prices rise and the dollars you have lose purchasing power. In other words, prices get inflated, and the value of the dollars you own goes down. There has been a secular decline in rates of year-over-year inflation in the United States since it peaked in June 1979, as you can see in Figure 17-3.

Now, imagine for a second, what would happen if everyone got UBI? This is basically free money, and everyone gets it. What would happen to the price of a cup of coffee, a car, clothes, or food if every single adult received a handout from the government for doing nothing? How much is a Honda when everyone is handed half a Honda in free income for doing nothing every year?

Figure 17-3: U.S. Consumer Price Inflation Rate[5]

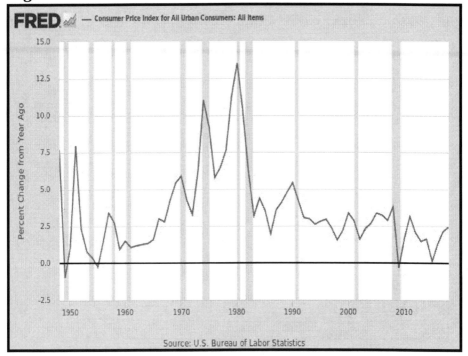

The logical outcome seems pretty straightforward: Prices would rise. Higher rates of inflation are good for asset holders and debt holders, but they are particularly bad for people on fixed income.

Fixed income investments include corporate bonds and Treasuries, as well as Social Security and defined benefits pensions. Given the risk of inflation from UBI, the minute people get UBI income and begin spending it, prices would rise, and those fixed income payments would be devalued.

As prices rise, the need to increase UBI would also rise to offset the loss of value from inflation. This would, in turn, send prices even higher, justifying the need to further increase UBI. And so forth and so on. So how much is enough? The truth is that once we go down the path of UBI, no amount may be enough. The printing presses of the future will need to digitally issue new money for UBI at an ever-quickening pace.

Low, stable inflation is conducive to growth, and high levels of inflation can make an economy unstable. If prices rise rapidly, as they did in Germany in the hyperinflation of the early 1920s, people could end up wallpapering their homes with worthless paper currency. To use a more recent example, paper bills could be denominated in the trillions, like they are in Zimbabwe.

Now, I'm not saying UBI would put us on the same path as 1920s Germany or modern-day Zimbabwe.

But I'm not saying it won't.

Taxes Would Rise

Since we cannot afford to pay for UBI with the current US government budget and we cannot afford to drive up our national debt by another $1 to $2 trillion (in today's value) annually, we would need to find the money for UBI somewhere else. We could just print it, but that means running up the debt; we can't surreptitiously run dollar printing presses, sneaking bags of UBI into everyone's home while they sleep like some kind of income Santa. But that is likely the plan most people are going with. Better stock up on milk and cookies now!

But in all seriousness, there is only one way to get the money that would be needed for UBI: taxes. It could be higher payroll taxes, higher corporate taxes, higher property taxes, or the creation of some new taxes, like a robotic labor payroll tax. But one thing is certain: Taxes would rise.

No matter what your view on UBI. we can probably all agree on one thing: Corporations (and individuals) respond to tax incentives. And higher taxes that are implemented to purely redistribute wealth without any labor or activity requirement on the part of the recipient would reduce incentives for technological development, investment, and economic activity.

Payroll Taxes on Robots

The debate about a payroll tax on robots has heated up, and a number of business leaders, including Bill Gates, have voiced support for such a policy. But defining which jobs are affected will be a challenge. Would it be for robots *and* computers? For hardware and software? For smartphones and Microsoft Excel?

The debate over a robot payroll tax is unlikely to go away, but its implementation, and the allocation of associated tax revenues, could be complicated. But a robot payroll tax is likely to be something that policymakers look at more closely over time, especially if a high number of jobs are automated out of existence.

Of course, the money from a robot payroll tax *could* be earmarked to fulfill the unfunded entitlement obligations of Medicare, Medicaid, and Social Security. After all, these are already funded by payroll taxes. But even with a robot payroll tax, policymakers may neglect to fund entitlement obligations, because if robot payroll taxes go to fund entitlements, there may not be much wiggle room to implement UBI.

Although I am very skeptical of the concepts of a robot payroll tax and universal basic income, one thing in the world of politics always rings true: When you rob Peter to pay Paul, you can always count on Paul's vote. In this case, Peter would be a robot without a vote. And Paul would get free money.

Corporate Taxes

As part of the U.S. tax reform of 2017, U.S. corporate tax rates were lowered. It was lauded as stimulative for corporate profits, for investments, and the economy. But a future move to significantly raise corporate tax rates to finance the UBI free handout for every American would likely meet with sharp resistance — and corporate relocations. The U.S. economy would likely experience a mass exodus of corporations that would seek to avoid UBI taxation. They would just leave.

Of course, we could single out technology corporations, but technology companies have a 5x multiplier on job creation [6]

Want to see the UBI needs balloon quickly? Scare away companies, where each job created is capable of supporting the creation of five additional jobs.

Taxes on Income Assets

Another way to finance UBI would be to tax people who work. Yes, everyone gets free UBI money. But the people who also get paid to work will pay for everyone else to get the UBI money — even if none of the other recipients work, want to work, or ever plan to work.

They will even pay UBI for the recipients who just want to play some future virtual reality holodeck version of Xbox their entire lives. This leads us to our next topic and the negative risks to long-term economic development from implementing such a UBI system.

Death and Taxes — or at Least Taxes

Before closing out this section, I want to note that there are currently two guarantees in life: death and taxes. Singularitarians and Transhumanists, like Zoltan Istvan, would tell you that death is not guaranteed in the future. In the future you may be able to live forever. However, taxes are still going to be guaranteed.

And with the implementation of UBI, *higher* taxes would also be guaranteed.

Negative Long-Run Economic Impacts

During the industrial revolution — at the onset of the age of iron and steel — factories decimated the occupations of smiths, weavers, and many others.

Of course, there were also very unpleasant times during the Industrial Revolution. There were widespread abuses of the labor force, including child labor, horrific working conditions, and a lack of worker protection.

This led to the creation of unions and resulted in labor reforms. Things like weekends, holidays, and paid vacations came from the development of unions, and a push toward more humane working environments proved to be successful as well.

These problems may have been imperfectly fixed, but society improved, and the economy progressed.

At the same time that village life was fully eroding, the emergence and creation of new professions also became critical. And broader access to university-level education helped train more doctors, journalists, lawyers, and other professionals. And there were great improvements across a number of professions and industries, which had very positive impacts on society.

But what would have happened if people had just stayed in their villages and they had just been given a handout?

Medieval Universal Basic Income

Imagine if 1000u European monarchs had decided to just hand out money to smiths, millers, and weavers to never work again. What would have happened to European growth? What if these tradesmen had managed to wrangle UBI out of the U.S. government in the late 1800s? What would have happened to the U.S. economy?

I suspect that such policies would have caused economies to suffer from significant underperformance, stifled economic development, and slow growth.

With such negative ramifications, why are people talking about UBI now?

UBI does not help individuals bridge skills gaps. It just avoids the problem by throwing money at it. But in doing so, it short circuits the adaptive nature of capitalist economies, and it reduces the longer-term potential for economic growth. This is something we need to think about in relation to UBI. If everyone just gets a handout, the economy will stop adapting — it will stop growing.

More importantly, there is an individual cost to UBI as a solution to permanent job loss. If individuals in the late 1800s had been given money because their jobs ceased to exist — because society had changed — what would have happened to those individual smiths, millers, tanners, and weavers if they had done nothing? Would they have also felt that they were nothing? What would have happened to society at that point? And what will happen to ours if people do nothing and receive UBI now?

German Shepherds

While a number of jobs over time are going to change and become obsolete, I fundamentally believe that humans will need things to do and that entire lives of unearned leisure are not exactly lives of pure contentment. Yes, a lot of years of leisure is nice. But have you ever wondered why billionaires continue to work? It's because they are German shepherds.

Most people I know — my family, close friends, and even acquaintances — remind me of German shepherds. They like to have things to do. They like to be busy and occupied. Anyone who has ever owned a German shepherd, watched a German shepherd, or volunteered in an animal shelter knows that if these dogs don't have enough to do, they'll destroy the furniture in their own house out of sheer boredom. It is my fundamental belief that people without enough to do will also rip up their own lives just to avoid being bored.

This is also a key lesson of Greek mythology. Greek gods and goddesses got into wars and conflicts because they were bored. With nothing to do, they wreaked havoc on the world for no reason other than sheer boredom. We should be concerned.

It's one thing when retirees receive entitlements, because they are generally less physically active. But it's another thing entirely when young adults are unoccupied; they need things to do. This could be a challenge in a future with more robots and automation. Without a way to keep people mentally and physically active, there are risks to society. It is a threat people don't think about — and they certainly don't talk about.

Idle hands are the work of the devil. For this reason, it is going to be a very big problem if people don't have something to do. A world without work — a world of UBI — presents existential risks to society. And this will impact finance as well.

As Kaplan pointed out in his book on robots and the future of work, *Humans Need Not Apply*, "Money is not the only reason to work. People like to feel that they are useful members of society. They enjoy making a contribution to the welfare of others in addition to providing for themselves and their families. Most people feel great satisfaction in helping others, increasing their sense of self-worth, and giving their lives purpose and meaning."[7]

Figure 17-4: Busy People are Happy People[8]

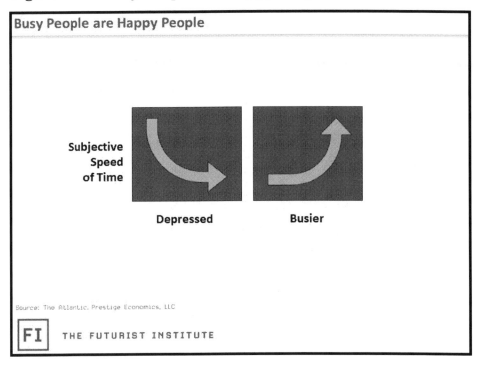

I have long said that busy people are happy people, which was a concept reinforced by an article in *The Atlantic* from February 2017, which included Figure 17-4.[9] Another *The Atlantic* writer noted that "The paradox of work is that many people hate their jobs, but they are considerably more miserable doing nothing."[10]

The Grandfather of Universal Basic Income

When the Berlin Wall fell in 1989 and the Soviet Union subsequently collapsed in 1991, the West declared that capitalism had defeated communism. But the view of history changes with time. After all, it is now accepted by most historians of European history that World War I and World War II were one war with a lengthy armistice between two periods of actual armed conflict. I must then wonder if we have actually seen the end of communism or if we are merely lodged in a period of armistice.

After all, if universal basic income makes it across the finish line of history, we may come to view the "end" of the Cold War as just Round 1 of a struggle that capitalism could still lose. I have read the works of communist leaders such as Marx, Engels, Lenin, Luxemburg, and Trotsky.

But some of their writings are less aggressive than the language used by some Silicon Valley executives when they speak about a post-capitalist Robotopia. Make no mistake: The final judgement on the failure of communism may not yet have been written. And while Bismarck is considered the grandfather of U.S. Social Security, I think we need to recognize that Karl Marx is the grandfather of universal basic income.

Figure 17-5: Grandfather of Universal Basic Income, Karl Marx[11]

The costs of universal basic income would be very high. UBI could lead to rampant inflation, an exodus of businesses, higher taxes, long-term economic stagnation, and a fracturing of individual lives and society. Universal basic income is not a viable choice. We must adapt to change.

Ascending Politics of Universal Basic Income
I first wrote about UBI in *Jobs for Robots* (2017). I subsequently had a number of interactions with proponents of UBI.

Many of these have been unpleasant.

Free money is an alluring offer, and I expected back in early 2017 that the number of people who think UBI is a great idea would rise sharply in the years to come. Back then, I noted that UBI is likely to be one of the hottest political issues of the coming two decades, to the point that it could well become a critical issue in elections for the U.S. presidency in short order.

Indeed, this expectation has already proven to be correct.

Right now, in 2019, we already have one presidential candidate touting the notion of UBI as a main part of his presidential campaign. For now, we have yet to see it be a main plank of multiple candidates running for president in the United States.

But I expect it will happen.

Even if the U.S. economy cannot afford it, free money for everyone would captivate a large swath of the American population.

UBI proponents could say, *"Non-workers of the world unite!"*

We must resist the siren song of free money because the false promise of UBI could sink the entire economy.

Unfortunately, however, universal basic income is likely to be a topic that will come to the fore in the United States and globally in the coming decade and beyond.

CHAPTER 18

GLOBAL UPSIDE OF FINTECH

One of the biggest potential positive economic impacts at the population level for FinTech isn't the marginal changes most banked individuals in developed economies could see in terms of lower costs and ease of use. The big promise of FinTech on a global scale is democratized access.

And the biggest value adds are likely to be — and remain — in emerging markets, where access to financial institutions, banks, and investments has historically been much more limited.

If you live in the United States or another OECD country, it may be difficult to understand that there is a massive number of unbanked individuals in emerging markets — let alone that there are some at home in the United States as well. But it's true.

Globally, 1.7 billion adults are unbanked. Furthermore, according to the World Bank, about half of these people live in just seven countries: Bangladesh, China, India, Indonesia, Mexico, Nigeria, and Pakistan. You can see the full map in Figure 18-1.[1]

Even in the United States, there are 8.4 million unbanked households. This means that about 6.5 percent of households are completely unbanked — and have no bank accounts of any kind — according to the Federal Deposit Insurance Corporation.[2]

Plus, there are an additional 24.2 million underbanked U.S. households. According to the FDIC, this means that 18.7 percent of all U.S. households. have "a checking or savings account but also obtained financial products and services outside of the banking system."[3]

This means that even in the United States, 33 million households — 25.2 percent of households — are unbanked or underbanked.

Figure 18-1: Number of Unbanked Adults Globally[4]

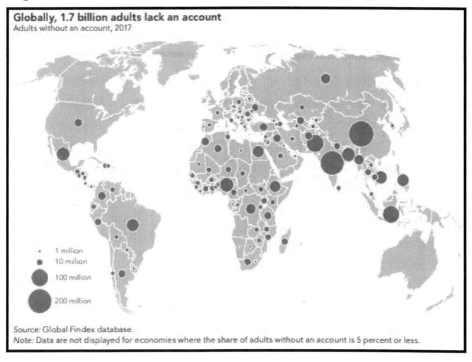

One of the main means to foster greater global access to finance is tied to tapping into the number of unbanked adults that have phones. According to the World Bank, two-thirds of unbanked adults have phones. And this offers promise for increasing the number of banked individuals, by using FinTech solutions that can reach those unbanked individuals through their phones.

In a June 2019 report, the IMF noted that FinTech is "having global impact on the provision of financial services" and that "mobile payments have been a key early developer with broad implications for inclusion." Among the big successes, the report explicitly underscored that Africa has seen "rapid growth in mobile money as a driver for greater financial inclusion."[5]

Figure 18-2: Two-Thirds of Unbanked Adults Have Phones[6]

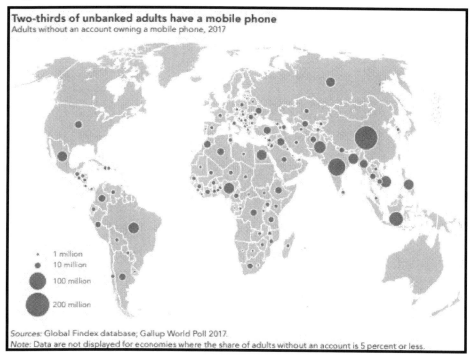

Two-thirds of unbanked adults have a mobile phone
Adults without an account owning a mobile phone, 2017

- 1 million
- 10 million
- 100 million
- 200 million

Sources: Global Findex database; Gallup World Poll 2017.
Note: Data are not displayed for economies where the share of adults without an account is 5 percent or less.

Similarly, the massive spread and adoption of mobile payments in Africa is also something that was highlighted in a 2017 World Bank report. There is a map of adoption showing the swift rise in the percent of adults in Sub-Saharan Africa that made mobile money accounts between 2014 and 2017 in Figure 18-3.

As we look at the future of FinTech, all eyes are on those unbanked and underbanked individuals in emerging markets — and at home. The future of finance will include bringing many of those individuals into the fold of banking, investments, and payments. And it is likely to be a critical priority for FinTech and traditional financial services companies developing or acquiring FinTech solutions to tap into that 1.7 billion person market.

Figure 18-3: Mobile Payments Spread in Africa[7]

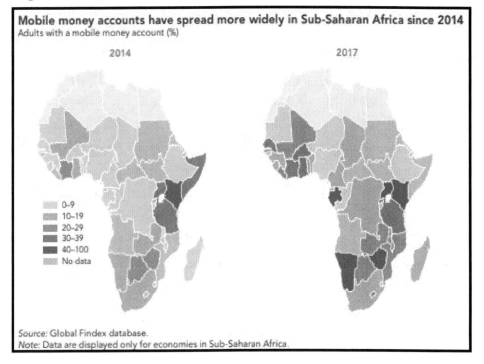

CHAPTER 19

ESG AND SUSTAINABILITY

One of the big trends for the future of finance is a push to incorporate environmental, social, and governance (ESG) goals along with sustainability. This is a trend that has been underway for some years and it is likely to increase and accelerate in the decade ahead — and beyond.

In 2018, some of the top areas where there were activist investors pushing for goals and initiatives included climate change (19%), sustainability (13%), other environmental (7%), and political activity (19%).[1] You can see the breakdown in Figure 19-1. If we consider sustainability a type of environmental initiative along with climate change and other environmental resolutions, we see that 39% — a plurality — of all activist investor resolutions filed in 2018 were environment related.

I want to be careful here on one point. I am not putting a value judgement on these resolutions. I merely wish to show that they were a plurality of activist investor resolutions in 2018 — and that they are likely to become increasingly common.

And they will become increasingly important in finance.

In short, activist investors are usually large investors that use their shareholder power to push companies to make fundamental changes in the way they operate.

And their activities have been on the rise. In fact, the number of companies subject to activist demands globally rose by almost 54 percent between 2013 and 2018. This can be seen in Figure 19-2.

Domestically, the situation is very similar, and the number of U.S. companies subject to activist demands is up by over 50 percent since 2013. This can be seen in Figure 19-3.

Figure 19-1: Type of Activist Resolutions Filed in 2018[2]

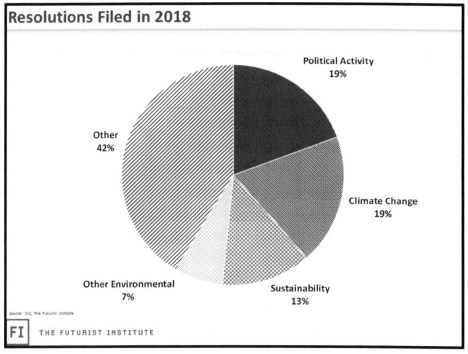

Figure 19-2: Global Companies Subject to Activist Demands[3]

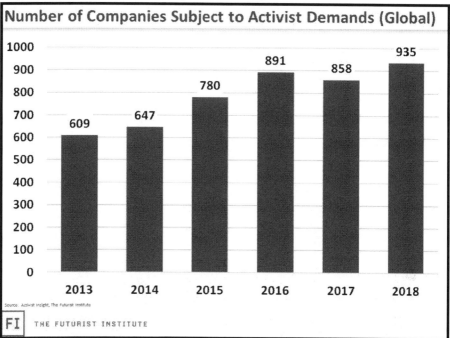

Figure 19-3: U.S. Companies Subject to Activist Demands[4]

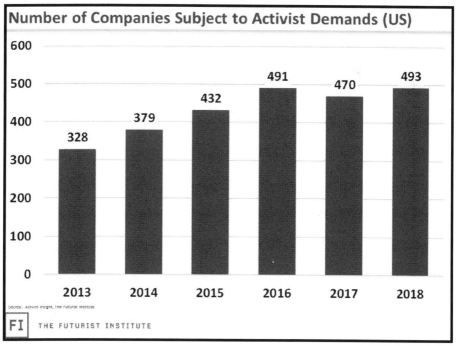

Looking at the future of finance, I expect that this dynamic of rising activist demands — and the number of companies impacted — is likely to continue rising on trend.

Any undergraduate economics student knows that companies often benefit from things they don't pay for but that have costs. These costs that are not captured but are passed on to society at large are called externalities. These include any potentially negative environmental impact a business's operations have. But they can also involve leveraging certain labor, societal, or political inefficiencies to capture an arbitrage opportunity to reap outsized financial benefits.

It should therefore not be a surprise that there has been a push to hold companies responsible for these externalities. After all, this is one of the very first things most economics students learn.

But here's the deal: Fully pricing in externalities to company operations is likely to erode profitability for some companies. And that may be just the beginning. Ratings agencies have already started warning companies I work with in the energy space that their sustainability goals (or lack thereof) could impact their bond prices and their weighted average cost of capital — their WACC.[5] This could in turn impact their profitability, overall valuation, credit rating, and equity prices.

In the future, companies will increasingly need to demonstrate achievable sustainability and other ESG goals. If they don't, they will be at the mercy of activist investors. And their profitability and share prices may very well suffer.

CHAPTER 20

THE IMPORTANCE OF TRADE

Nationalist politics present risks of isolationist trade policies, which could significantly impact supply chains globally. We have already started to see these dynamics, especially in the United States.

Additional trade restrictions to protect national interests above international interests are a major risk across the global economy. Furthermore, these risks are likely to remain in play for the United States and other economies.

These kinds of trade risks became a major red flag for the International Monetary Fund in 2018, due in large part because very strong global growth in 2017 was attributed to strong global trade. If trade conflicts continue and proliferate further, the downside risks to overall global economic growth will increase.

To put these risks in perspective, trade risks were on no one's radar as a major risk of any kind in 2015. Very few analysts considered them to be credible risks well into 2018, even after U.S. Section 232 and 301 tariffs were announced.

Equity markets also took big hits in the past year and a half when trade was at risk, particularly around the U.S.-China trade war Markets often fell through critical technical supports, causing technical selloffs to follow fundamental selloffs on trade risks.

Of course, equity markets often rebounded at times when the outlook for the U.S.-China trade conflict improved. This had a similar impact of pushing markets above technical buy levels and engendering technical rallies that followed fundamentally bullish ones. In short, trade uncertainty has added market volatility.

As we consider the importance of trade for the future of finance, I believe it is important to recognize that global economic growth is highly sensitive to global trade. And there are broader global macroeconomic risks of economic deceleration, destabilization, and even recession in a high-risk trade environment.

At the time this book went to print, the economic expansion since the Great Recession of 2007-2009 was the longest in American history. But trade wars could dampen the outlook significantly.

As Ben Bernanke noted on 4 January 2019 at a panel with Fed Chair Powell and fellow Fed Chair Yellen, business cycles don't die of old age; they get murdered. In other words, economic expansions usually end because of something overlooked that creates a shock to the economic system. Trade is a big risk to the current cycle. And trade is likely to remain a critical factor for global growth for the future of financial markets and the economy — just as it always has in the past.

THE FUTURE OF FINANCE
IS NOW

My main goal in writing this book was to share my view on the future of finance, including how markets, technology, risks, and global dynamics are likely to play out in the decade ahead and beyond.

Hopefully, you now have an understanding of some of the top-line risks and opportunities ahead for financial services, FinTech, and financial markets.

The disruptive nature of the trends that are already underway will play out in impactful ways for individuals, companies, and entire industries. Perhaps the most disruptive impact will be in the composition of the financial company of the future.

In short, there will be a lot more people focused on technology, and there will be far fewer people doing what we think of as traditional financial services jobs. This will impact banking, insurance, financial planning, and the rest. You can see one forecast of the impact on financial services jobs in Figure 21-1.

In many of the books I have written, I have often noted that the companies that will survive and thrive in the current and future era of disruptive technological innovations will be at their heart technology companies. This appears to be the path forward for financial services as well.

Historically speaking, education has been the great divider for jobs. In Figure 21-2, you can see statistics on unemployment and earnings from 2018 from the U.S. Bureau of Labor Statistics. Education is positively correlated with income, and education is also inversely correlated with unemployment. In other words, generally speaking, the more education you have, the more money you make and the lower the chance you are unemployed.

Figure 21-1: Forecasted Financial Institution Staff Reductions[1]

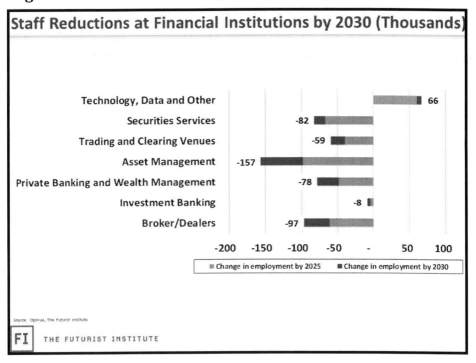

Looking ahead to the future of finance, we still expect that education will remain a critical deciding factor that impacts employability and wages — even if disruption and a massive job shake-up comes to the financial world. But those future job opportunities may be in different areas. And people will need to rely on their ability to learn new, more technology-focused skills to push their careers forward.

Additionally, it is important to note that some parts of high finance will very much remain a closed network in which education and other accoutrements of professional achievement are conditio sine qua non to be a part of the game. In other words, for some parts of finance, FinTech will not be a substitute.

Figure 21-2: Education, Earnings, and Unemployment[2]

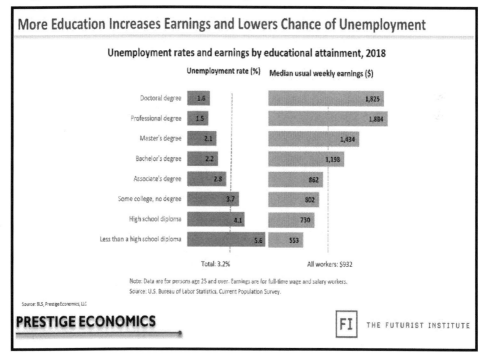

Further Learning

If you've enjoyed this book and want to learn more about the future of finance and how to incorporate new and emerging technology risks and opportunities into your strategic planning, you may want to pursue the Certified Futurist and Long-Term Analyst™ — FLTA™ — training program that I created for The Futurist Institute.

The FLTA™ certification program has six distinct professional tracks, including a financial planning track and an accounting and tax track. Plus, The Futurist Institute is accredited by the Certified Financial Planner Board of Standards® as a provider of continuing education hours. And the FLTA program includes 8.5 hours of CFP® continuing education.

All of the details about the FLTA™ and The Futurist Institute can be found at www.futuristinstitute.org.

Your Next Steps

The future of finance will bring opportunities, risks, and challenges. But now that you have been informed of some of the biggest trends that will drive financial services, FinTech, and financial markets in the decade ahead, you can take action.

You are the master of your own destiny, and it's up to you to stay one step ahead of the crowd. Because if you do, there could be big rewards in store. After all, in finance, money is made at the margin. And you've got more than a little edge.

Plus, the future of finance is *now*!

ENDNOTES

Chapter 4

1. "Listed Domestic Companies, Total." *Data*, World Bank, data.worldbank.org/indicator/CM.MKT.LDOM.NO?locations=US.
2. Ritter, Jay R. (9 April 2019). "IPO Data." *Warrington College of Business*, University of Florida. Retrieved on 12 July 2019 from site.warrington.ufl.edu/ritter/ipo-data/.
3. Ibid.
4. Ibid.
5. Ibid.
6. Ibid.

Chapter 7

1. "Widespread Fraud Found in Cryptocurrency Offerings." (April 10, 2018). Texas State Securities Board. Retrieved on 24 August 2018 from https://www.ssb.texas.gov/sites/default/files/CRYPTO%20report%20April%2010%202018.pdf.
2. "Bitcoin (USD) Price." Coindesk. Retrieved on 24 August 2018 from https://www.coindesk.com/price/.
3. "What is Bitcoin? Google Trends Search" Google Trends. Retrieved on 24 August 2018 from https://trends.google.com/trends/explore?q=What%20is%20Bitcoin%3F&geo=US.
4. Katz, L. (1 August 2018). "Long Blockchain Gets Hit With SEC Subpoena After Nasdaq Ouster." Bloomberg News. Retrieved on 24 August 2018 from https://www.bloomberg.com/news/articles/2018-08-01/long-blockchain-gets-hit-with-sec-subpoena-after-nasdaq-ouster.

Chapter 8

1. Speech by Darryl Willis, VP Oil, Gas, and Energy, Google Cloud at Google. Speech given at D2:Upheaval on 10 October 2018.
2. *Investopedia*. "Moore's Law." Retrieved on 7 November 2018 from https://www.investopedia.com/terms/m/mooreslaw.asp.
3. Gribbin, J. *Computing with Quantum Cats: From Colossus to Qubits*. Prometheus Books: New York. p. 92.
4. Jurvetson, S. (10 December 2016). "Moore's Law Over 120 Years." Flickr. Retrieved on 1 November 2018 from https://www.flickr.com/photos/jurvetson/31409423572/.
5. Speech by Deepu Talla, Vice President and General Manager of Autonomous Machines, NVIDIA, at RoboBusiness on 26 September 2018.
6. Tovey, A (2 April 2014). "When Milliseconds Mean Millions." *The Telegraph*. Retrieved on 12 July 2019 from https://www.telegraph.co.uk/finance/newsbysector/banksandfinance/10736960/High-frequency-trading-when-milliseconds-mean-millions.html.

Chapter 9

1. *FinTech Survey Report* (April 2016). CFA Institute. Retrieved February 11, 2017: https://www.cfainstitute.org/Survey/fintech_survey.PDF.
2. Szmigiera, M. (13 March 2019). "Number of ETFs Worldwide 2003-2017." *Statista*, Statista, www.statista.com/statistics/278249/global-number-of-etfs/.

Chapter 10

1. Pur lup i Ai (MUAU). "Diair Dondr From Rupul ir to Prohibited" Investopedia. Retrieved on 24 August 2018 from https://www.investopedia.com/articles/bonds/08/bearer-bond.asp.
2. Image provided courtesy of Heritage Auctions, HA.com. Retrieved on 24 August 2018 from https://currency.ha.com/itm/miscellaneous/other/-1-000-000-us-treasury-bearer-bond/a/364-15547.s.
3. Lagarde, C (26 April 2018). "Statement by IMF Managing Director Christine Lagarde on Her Participation in the Paris Conference on Terrorism Financing." International Monetary Fund. Retrieved on 24 August 2018 from https://www.imf.org/en/News/Articles/2018/04/26/pr18150-lagarde-on-her-participation-in-the-paris-conference-on-terrorism-financing.
4. "Annual Economics Report." (June 2018). Bank of International Settlements, p. 91-141. Retrieved from https://www.bis.org/publ/arpdf/ar2018e.pdf.
5. Powell, J. "Semiannual Monetary Policy Report to the Congress." U.S. Federal Reserve. Retrieved on 12 July 2019 from https://www.federalreserve.gov/newsevents/testimony/powell20190710a.htm.

Chapter 12

1. Delfs, H., Knebl, H. (2015). *Introduction to Cryptography: Principles and Applications.* Third Edition. Springer: New York. P. 343.
2. Ibid. P. 350.
3. Decker, Susan, and Yasiejko Christopher. (2018). "Forget the Trade War. China Wants to Win Computing Arms Race." Bloomberg.com, Bloomberg, 9 April 2018, www.bloomberg.com/news/articles/2018-04-08/forget-the-trade-war-china-wants-to-win-the-computing-arms-race.
4. US Trade Representative Report. Pp. 10-11. Retrieved on 6 November 2018 from USTR at https://ustr.gov/sites/default/files/Section%20301%20FINAL.PDF.
5. Several of Navarro's books offer insight into US-China policies.
6. "2018 Cost of a Data Breach Study: Global Overview." (July 2018). Ponemon Institute LLC. IBM, p. 13. Retrieved on 25 October 2018 from https://public.dhe.ibm.com/common/ssi/ecm/55/en/55017055usen/2018-global-codb-report_06271811_55017055USEN.pdf.
7. "Internet Security Threat Report." (March 2018). Symantec, Symantec Corporation, p. 9. Retrieved on 25 October 2018 from http://images.mktgassets.symantec.com/Web/Symantec/%7B3a70beb8-c55d-4516-98ed-1d0818a42661%7D_ISTR23_Main-FINAL-APR10.pdf?aid=elq
8. de Wolf, R. (2017). "The Potential Impact of Quantum Computers on Society," p. 2.
9. US Congress. (2018), "Cybersecurity Funding." White House, p. 274. Retrieved on 25 October 2018 from https://www.whitehouse.gov/wp-content/uploads/2018/02/ap_21_cyber_security-fy2019.pdf.
10. "Risk Nexus: Overcome by Cyber Risks? Economic Benefits and Costs of Alternate Cyber Futures." (2015) Atlantic Council, Zurich Insurance Group, p. 11. Retrieved on 25 October 2018 from http://publications.atlanticcouncil.org/cyberrisks/risk-nexus-september-2015-overcome-by-cyber-risks.pdf.

Chapter 14

1. Rodriguez, A. (24 March 2016) "Microsoft's AI millennial chatbot became a racist jerk after less than a day on Twitter." Quartz. Retrieved February 17, 2017: https://qz.com/646825/microsofts-ai-millennial-chatbot-became-a-racist-jerk-after-less-than-a-day-on-twitter/

Chapter 15

1. Most recently Fed Chair Powell noted this risk in July 2019 before Congress. Powell, J. "Semiannual Monetary Policy Report to the Congress." U.S. Federal Reserve. Retrieved on 12 July 2019 from https://www.federalreserve.gov/newsevents/testimony/powell20190710a.htm.
2. Retrieved from http://www.usdebtclock.org/

3. U.S. Department of the Treasury. Fiscal Service, Federal Debt: Total Public Debt [GFDEBTN], retrieved from FRED, Federal Reserve Bank of St. Louis; https://fred.stlouisfed.org/series/GFDEBTN, 17 June 2019.

4. Ibid.

5. Federal Reserve Bank of St. Louis and US Office of Management and Budget, Federal Debt: Total Public Debt as Percent of Gross Domestic Product [GFDEGDQ188S], retrieved from FRED, Federal Reserve Bank of St. Louis; https://fred.stlouisfed.org/series/GFDEGDQ188S, 17 June 2019.

6. Desjardins, J. (6 August 2015). "$60 Trillion of World Debt in One Visualization." Visual Capitalist. Retrieved 11 February 2017: http://www.visualcapitalist.com/60-trillion-of-world-debt-in-one-visualization/.

7. Mayer, J. (18 November 2015). "The Social Security Façade." Retrieved 11 February 2017: http://www.usnews.com/opinion/economic-intelligence/2015/11/18/social-security-and-medicare-have-morphed-into-unsustainable-entitlements.

8. U.S. Social Security Administration. "Social Security History: Otto von Bismarck." Sourced from https://www.ssa.gov/history/ottob.html.

9. Image provided courtesy of The Heritage Foundation. Retrieved 11 February 2017: http://thf_media.s3.amazonaws.com/infographics/2014/10/BG-eliminate-waste-control-spending-chart-3_HIGHRES.jpg.

10. Twarog, S. (January 1997). "Heights and Living Standards in Germany, 1850-1939: The Case of Wurttemberg" as reprinted in *Health and Welfare During Industrialization.* Steckel, R. and F. Roderick, eds. Chicago: University of Chicago Press, p. 315. Retrieved 11 February 2017: http://www.nber.org/chapters/c7434.pdf.

11. U.S. Social Security Administration. "Social Security History: Otto von Bismarck." Sourced from https://www.ssa.gov/history/ottob.html.

12. U.S. Social Security Administration. *Fast Facts and Figures About Social Security, 2017,* p. 8. Retrieved on 17 June 2019: https://www.ssa.gov/policy/docs/chartbooks/fast_facts/.

13. World Bank, Population Growth for the United States [SPPOPGROWUSA], retrieved from FRED, Federal Reserve Bank of St. Louis; https://fred.stlouisfed.org/series/SPPOPGROWUSA, June 5, 2018.

14. Last, J. (2013) *What to Expect, When No One's Expecting: America's Coming Demographic Disaster.* New York: Encounter Books, pp. 2-4.

15. Ibid., p. 3.

16. Last (2013), p. 109.

17. U.S. Social Security Administration. Retrieved 11 February 2017 from https://www.ssa.gov/history/ratios.html Last (2013) also uses a similar table in his book on p. 108.

18. Last (2013), p. 107.

19. Trading Economics. Spanish unemployment. Retrieved February 2017 http://www.tradingeconomics.com/spain/unemployment-rate.

20. Trading Economics. Spanish unemployment. Retrieved February 2017 http://www.tradingeconomics.com/spain/youth-unemployment-rate.

21. U.S. Internal Revenue Service. Retrieved from https://www.irs.gov/businesses/small-businesses-self-employed/self-employment-tax-social-security-and-medicare-taxes.

22. Pew Research Center. (22 October 2015). Retrieved 19 February 2017: http://www.pewsocialtrends.org/2015/10/22/three-in-ten-u-s-jobs-are-held-by-the-self-employed-and-the-workers-they-hire/.

23. Ibid.

Chapter 16

1. "Genesis Block." Wikipedia. Bitcoin Wiki. Retrieved on 24 August 2018 from https://en.bitcoin.it/wiki/Main_Page

2. Bank of England, Total Central Bank Assets for United Kingdom (DISCONTINUED) [UKASSETS], retrieved from FRED, Federal Reserve Bank of St. Louis; https://fred.stlouisfed.org/series/UKASSETS, 24 August 2018.

3. European Central Bank, Central Bank Assets for Euro Area (11-19 Countries) [ECBASSETS], retrieved from FRED, Federal Reserve Bank of St. Louis; https://fred.stlouisfed.org/series/ECBASSETS, 12 July 2019.

4. "Balance Sheets of the Bank of Japan and Financial Institutions." Bank of Japan, Retrieved on 24 August 2018 from https://www.boj.or.jp/en/statistics/category/financial.htm/.

5. Ujikane, K. and Toshiro H. (16 April 2019)."Veteran Investor With Family Pedigree Slams BOJ's ETF Buying." *Bloomberg.com*, Bloomberg. Retrieved on 12 July 2019 from www.bloomberg.com/news/articles/2019-04-15/veteran-fund-manager-with-family-pedigree-slams-boj-s-etf-buying. This also involved data from "BOJ's ETF Purchases Expanding Steadily" Japan Center for Economic Research. Retrieved on 12 July 2019 from https://www.jcer.or.jp/eng/pdf/170706_report (eng).pdf.

6. Board of Governors of the Federal Reserve System (US), All Federal Reserve Banks: Total Assets [WALCL], retrieved from FRED, Federal Reserve Bank of St. Louis; https://fred.stlouisfed.org/series/WALCL, 12 July 2019.

7. Yellen, J. (26 August 2016). *"The Federal Reserve's Monetary Policy Toolkit: Past, Present, and Future."* US Federal Reserve. Retrieved from https://www.federalreserve.gov/newsevents/speech/yellen20160826a.htm

Chapter 17

1. Freedman, D. (2016 July/August). "Basic Income: A Sellout of the American Dream." *MIT Technology Review*, p. 52.

2. Ibid., 53.

3. Gentilini, U. (11 January 2017). "Why Universal Basic Income is a Simple, but Effective Idea." World Bank as reprinted by the World Economic Forum. Retrieved 11 February 2017: https://www.weforum.org/agenda/2017/01/in-a-complex-world-the-apparent-simplicity-of-universal-basic-income-is-appealing.

4. Ibid.

5. U.S. Bureau of Labor Statistics, Consumer Price Index for All Urban Consumers: All Items [CPIAUCSL], retrieved on 15 July 2019 from FRED, Federal Reserve Bank of St. Louis; https://fred.stlouisfed.org/series/CPIAUCSL.

6. Moretti, E. (2013). *The New Geography of Jobs.* New York: Mariner Books, p. 13.

7. Kaplan, J. (2015), 184-185.

8. Hamblin, J. (2 February 2017) "How to Make Time Pass Quickly," *The Atlantic*: https://www.theatlantic.com/health/archive/2017/02/how-to-make-time-move/515361/

9. Ibid.

10. Thompson, D. (2015 July/August). "A World Without Work," *The Atlantic*. Retrieved from https://www.theatlantic.com/magazine/archive/2015/07/world-without-work/395294/

11. Image licensed from Adobe Stock.

Chapter 18

1. World Bank. Retrieved on 12 July 2019 from https://globalfindex.worldbank.org/.
2. "2017 FDIC National Survey of Unbanked and Underbanked Households." Federal Deposit Insurance Corporation. Retrieved on 12 July 2019 from https://www.fdic.gov/householdsurvey/. "The Global Findex Database: Measuring Financial Inclusion and the Fintech Revolution." (2017).
3. Ibid.
4. World Bank. Retrieved on 12 July 2019 from https://globalfindex.worldbank.org/.
5. "Fintech: The Experience So Far." (27 June 2019). International Monetary Fund.
6. World Bank. Retrieved on 12 July 2019 from https://globalfindex.worldbank.org/.
7. Ibid.

Chapter 19

1. Welsh, H. (9 November 2018). "Social, Environmental & Sustainable Governance Shareholder Proposals in 2018." *Securities and Exchange Commission*, Sustainable Investments Institute. Retrieved on 12 July 2019 from www.sec.gov/comments/4-725/4725-4636528-176443.pdf.
2. Ibid.
3. "Shareholder Activism in Q1 2019." (April 2019). *Reports*. Activist Insight. Retrieved on 12 July 2019 from www.activistinsight.com/research/ShareholderActivism_Q12019.pdf.
4. Ibid.
5. This comes on the heels of pressure from activist investor pushes on the Exxon board for a lack of ESG oversight. "Exxon Board Targeted for Lack of ESG Oversight." (May 11, 2019). National Association of Corporate Directors. Retrieved on 12 July 2019 https://tinyurl.com/NACDExxon2019.

Conclusion

1. Pierron, A. (16 May 2019). "Workforce of the Future: Transplanting Technology Skill Sets to the Capital Markets." Opimas. Retrieved on 13 July from www.opimas.com/research/472/detail/.
2. "Unemployment Rates and Earnings by Educational Attainment, 2018." (2019.) U.S. Bureau of Labor Statistics. Retrieved on 13 July 2019 from https://www.bls.gov/emp/chart-unemployment-earnings-education.htm.

ABOUT THE AUTHOR

Jason Schenker is the Chairman of The Futurist Institute, the President of Prestige Economics, and the world's top-ranked financial market futurist. Bloomberg News has ranked Mr. Schenker the #1 forecaster in the world in 25 categories since 2011, including for his forecasts of crude oil prices, natural gas prices, the euro, the pound, the Swiss franc, the Chinese RMB, gold prices, industrial metals prices, agricultural prices, U.S. non-farm payrolls, and U.S. new home sales.

Mr. Schenker has written 17 books and edited two almanacs. Five of his books have been #1 Bestsellers on Amazon, including *Commodity Prices 101*, *Recession-Proof*, *Electing Recession*, *Quantum: Computing Nouveau*, and *Jobs for Robots*. He also edited the #1 Bestseller *The Robot and Automation Almanac — 2018* as well as the 2019 edition of the almanac. Mr. Schenker is also a columnist for *Bloomberg Opinion*, and he has appeared as a guest host on Bloomberg Television as well as a guest on CNBC and other television media. He is frequently quoted in the press, including *The Wall Street Journal*, *The New York Times*, and *The Financial Times*.

Prior to founding Prestige Economics, Mr. Schenker worked for McKinsey & Company as a risk specialist, where he directed trading and risk initiatives on six continents. Before joining McKinsey, Mr. Schenker worked for Wachovia as an economist.

Mr. Schenker holds a Master's in Applied Economics from UNC Greensboro, a Master's in Negotiation from CSU Dominguez Hills, a Master's in German from UNC Chapel Hill, and a Bachelor's with distinction in History and German from The University of Virginia. He also holds a certificate in FinTech from MIT, an executive certificate in Supply Chain Management from MIT, a graduate certificate in Professional Development from UNC, a certificate in Negotiation from Harvard Law School, and a certificate in Cybersecurity from Carnegie Mellon University.

Mr. Schenker holds the professional designations ERP™ (Energy Risk Professional), CMT® (Chartered Market Technician), CVA® (Certified Valuation Analyst), CFP® (Certified Financial Planner), and FLTA™ (Certified Futurist and Long-Term Analyst). Mr. Schenker is also an instructor for LinkedIn Learning. His courses include Financial Risk Management, Recession-Proof Strategies, Audit and Due Diligence, and a weekly Economic Indicator Series.

Mr. Schenker is a member of the Texas Business Leadership Council, the only CEO-based public policy research organization in Texas, with a limited membership of 100 CEOs and Presidents. He is also a 2018 Board of Director member of the Texas Lyceum, a non-partisan, nonprofit that fosters business and policy dialogue on important U.S. and Texas issues. He is also the VP of Technology for the Texas Lyceum Executive Committee.

Mr. Schenker is an active executive in FinTech. He has been a member of the Central Texas Angel Network, and he advises multiple startups and nonprofits. He is also a member of the National Association of Corporate Directors as well as an NACD Board Governance Fellow.

In October 2016, Mr. Schenker founded The Futurist Institute to help consultants, strategists, and executives become futurists through an online and in-person training and certification program. Participants can earn the Certified Futurist and Long-Term Analyst™ — FLTA™ — designation.

Mr. Schenker was ranked one of the top 100 most influential financial advisors in the world by Investopedia in June 2018.

More information about Jason Schenker:
www.jasonschenker.com

More information about The Futurist Institute:
www.futuristinstitute.org

More information about Prestige Economics:
www.prestigeeconomics.com

TOP FORECASTER ACCURACY RANKINGS

Prestige Economics has been recognized as the most accurate independent commodity and financial market research firm in the world. As the only forecaster for Prestige Economics, Jason Schenker is very proud that Bloomberg News has ranked him a top forecaster in 43 different categories since 2011, including #1 in the world in 25 different forecast categories.

Mr. Schenker has been top ranked as a forecaster of economic indicators, energy prices, metals prices, agricultural prices, and foreign exchange rates.

ECONOMICS TOP RANKINGS
#1 Non-Farm Payroll Forecaster in the World
#1 New Home Sales Forecaster in the World
#2 U.S. Unemployment Rate Forecaster in the World
#3 Durable Goods Orders Forecaster in the World
#6 Consumer Confidence Forecaster in the World
#7 ISM Manufacturing Index Forecaster in the World
#7 U.S. Housing Start Forecaster in the World

ENERGY PRICE TOP RANKINGS

#1 WTI Crude Oil Price Forecaster in the World

#1 Brent Crude Oil Price Forecaster in the World

#1 Henry Hub Natural Gas Price Forecaster in the World

METALS PRICE TOP RANKINGS

#1 Gold Price Forecaster in the World

#1 Platinum Price Forecaster in the World

#1 Palladium Price Forecaster in the World

#1 Industrial Metals Price Forecaster in the World

#1 Copper Price Forecaster in the World

#1 Aluminum Price Forecaster in the World

#1 Nickel Price Forecaster in the World

#1 Tin Price Forecaster in the World

#1 Zinc Price Forecaster in the World

#2 Precious Metals Price Forecaster in the World

#2 Silver Price Forecaster in the World

#2 Lead Price Forecaster in the World

#2 Iron Ore Forecaster in the World

AGRICULTURAL PRICE TOP RANKINGS

#1 Coffee Price Forecaster in the World

#1 Cotton Price Forecaster in the World

#1 Sugar Price Forecaster in the World

#1 Soybean Price Forecaster in the World

FOREIGN EXCHANGE TOP RANKINGS

#1 Euro Forecaster in the World

#1 British Pound Forecaster in the World

#1 Swiss Franc Forecaster in the World

#1 Chinese RMB Forecaster in the World

#1 Russian Ruble Forecaster in the World

#1 Brazilian Real Forecaster in the World

#2 Turkish Lira Forecaster in the World

#3 Major Currency Forecaster in the World

#3 Canadian Dollar Forecaster in the World

#4 Japanese Yen Forecaster in the World

#5 Australian Dollar Forecaster in the World

#7 Mexican Peso Forecaster in the World

#1 EURCHF Forecaster in the World

#2 EURJPY Forecaster in the World

#2 EURGBP Forecaster in the World

#2 EURRUB Forecaster in the World

More information about Prestige Economics:

www.prestigeeconomics.com

----------- **PUBLISHER** -----------

Prestige Professional Publishing was founded in 2011 to produce insightful and timely professional reference books. We are registered with the Library of Congress.

Published Titles

Be the Shredder, Not the Shred
Commodity Prices 101
Electing Recession
Financial Risk Management Fundamentals
Futureproof Supply Chain
A Gentle Introduction to Audit and Due Diligence
Jobs for Robots
Midterm Economics
Quantum: Computing Nouveau
Robot-Proof Yourself
Spikes: Growth Hacking Leadership
The Dumpster Fire Election
The Fog of Data
The Future of Energy
The Future of Finance is Now
The Promise of Blockchain
The Robot and Automation Almanac — 2018
The Robot and Automation Almanac — 2019

Future Titles

Reading the Economic Tea Leaves
The Future of Agriculture
The Future of Healthcare
The Robot and Automation Almanac — 2020

Jobs for Robots provides an in-depth look at the future of automation and robots, with a focus on the opportunities as well as the risks ahead. Job creation in coming years will be extremely strong for the kind of workers that do not require payroll taxes, health care, or vacation: robots. *Jobs for Robots* was published in February 2017. This book has been a #1 Best Seller on Amazon.

The Fog of Data addresses the rising volume of data and describes the best ways to navigate data challenges — and how to derive valuable data insights. *The Fog of Data* was published by Prestige Professional Publishing in March 2019.

FROM THE AUTHOR

The following disclaimer applies to any content in this book:

This book is commentary intended for general information use only and is not investment advice. Jason Schenker does not make recommendations on any specific or general investments, investment types, asset classes, non-regulated markets, specific equities, bonds, or other investment vehicles. Jason Schenker does not guarantee the completeness or accuracy of analyses and statements in this book, nor does Jason Schenker assume any liability for any losses that may result from the reliance by any person or entity on this information. Opinions, forecasts, and information are subject to change without notice. This book does not represent a solicitation or offer of financial or advisory services or products; this book is only market commentary intended and written for general information use only. This book does not constitute investment advice. All links were correct and active at the time this book was published.

DISCLAIMER

FROM THE PUBLISHER

The following disclaimer applies to any content in this book:

This book is commentary intended for general information use only and is not investment advice. Prestige Professional Publishing, LLC does not make recommendations on any specific or general investments, investment types, asset classes, non-regulated markets, specific equities, bonds, or other investment vehicles. Prestige Professional Publishing, LLC does not guarantee the completeness or accuracy of analyses and statements in this book, nor does Prestige Professional Publishing, LLC assume any liability for any losses that may result from the reliance by any person or entity on this information. Opinions, forecasts, and information are subject to change without notice. This book does not represent a solicitation or offer of financial or advisory services or products; this book is only market commentary intended and written for general information use only. This book does not constitute investment advice. All links were correct and active at the time this book was published.

Prestige Professional Publishing, LLC

7101 Fig Vine Cove

Austin, Texas 78750

www.prestigeprofessionalpublishing.com

ISBN: **978-1-946197-34-4** *Paperback*

978-1-946197-33-7 *Ebook*

Made in the USA
Columbia, SC
24 July 2019